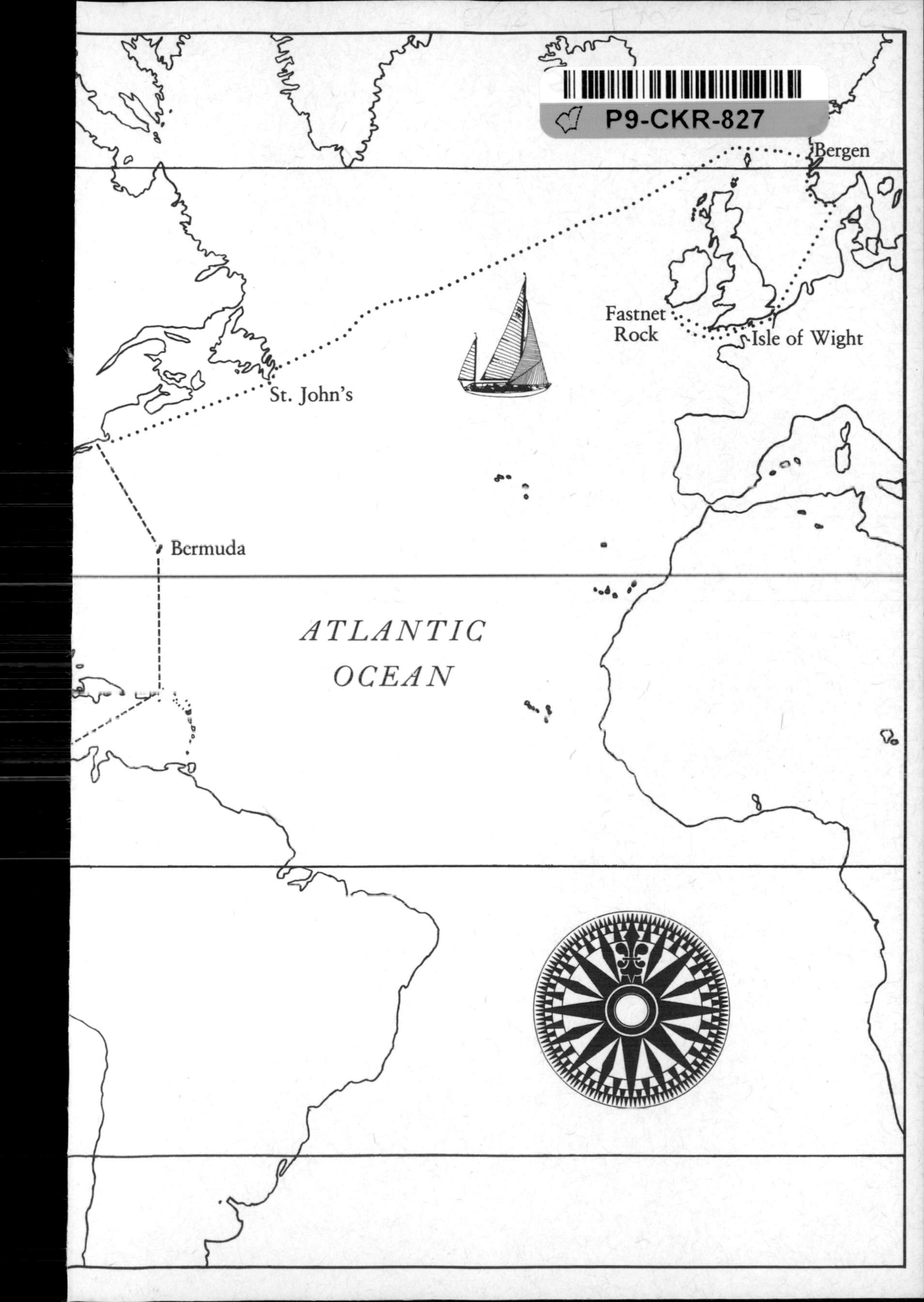
P9-CKR-827
Bergen
Fastnet Rock
Isle of Wight
St. John's
Bermuda
ATLANTIC
OCEAN

Loki and Loon

Loki & Loon

A Lifetime Affair with the Sea

Gifford B. Pinchot

A Triton Book

DODD, MEAD & COMPANY
New York

Published by Dodd, Mead & Company, Inc.
79 Madison Avenue, New York, N.Y. 10016
Distributed in Canada by
McClelland and Stewart Limited, Toronto
Manufactured in the United States of America

Library of Congress Cataloging in Publication Data

Pinchot, Gifford B.
Loki and Loon: a lifetime affair with the sea.

1. Yachts and yachting. 2. Sailing. I. Title.
GV813.P56 1985 797.1 85-6907
ISBN 0-396-08678-0

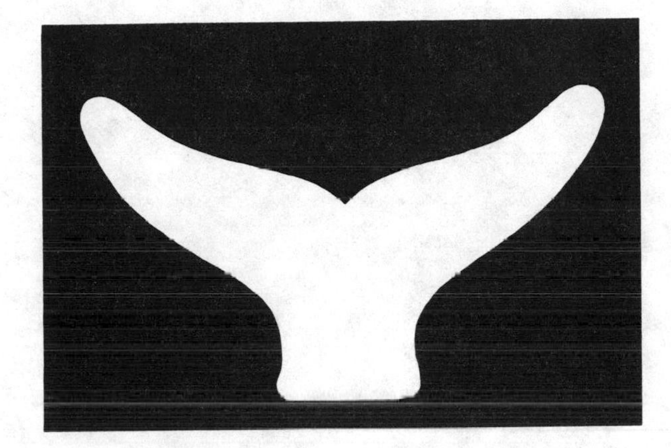

Dedication

To Sally

She was described by Ev Morris in an introduction to a chapter she wrote in *Racing at Sea* as "a young woman who just about epitomizes the yachtsman's dream of a perfect wife." I couldn't agree more. This is really Sally's book more than mine, since it is written from the logs she kept, illustrated by the pictures she took, and has even been edited by her into acceptable English. She is never daunted by discomfort or danger and is always enthusiastic about taking on further adventures. She is a superb navigator, both coastwise and celestial; an indomitable cook, no matter how foul the weather; has a wonderful sense of humor, no matter how bad the going; and is never too tired to take on more than her share of the work. Who could have the gall to ask for all this in one wife?

The true peace of God begins at any point
1000 miles from the nearest land.

—Joseph Conrad

Prologue

June 29, 1981, 1630 GMT, lat. 42° 51′N, long. 11° 10′W.

Sally is in the forecastle feeding the pigeon that came aboard near Ushant, the British name for the Ile d'Ouessant, off the coast of Brittany. She has just cleaned the cage, which she made out of the wastebasket from the head, and lined it with old charts, as we have run out of newspaper. We have the pigeon down below in a cage because conditions have gotten too wild for her on deck. She was blown overboard twice, and was just barely able to get airborne again and fly back to her slippery perch on the top of the dinghy amidships.

Dick is in the galley starting supper. Briggs, off watch, has his nose in a book, and Bill is in the upper bunk having a snooze. I've gotten the tape recorder out to record the roar of the wind in the rigging. There's a loud crash as the top of a sea comes aboard. Some of it finds its way down the companionway, damping down the cook, who asks, "Where the hell is that slide we were going to put in the companionway?" The tape records it all.

It was late in the afternoon, and *Loon* was charging along in a gale about a hundred miles west of Cape Finisterre on the northwest coast of Spain, on her way home from a two-year cruise to Ireland, Scotland, and Scandinavia. The wind had shifted from northwest to northeast, leaving a confused, steep sea that gave us a rough and decidedly wet sleigh ride on our southerly course. Running downwind, even under shortened sail, *Loon* had gotten a bit hard to steer. We were all tired after having been out for only four days from Falmouth, England, and were not yet thoroughly into the swing of life at sea. The going had been wild and exciting, but the prospect of running with the gale all night, with maybe more wind to come, was more than we wanted, tired as we were. So, with a storm trysail set and a storm staysail trimmed to weather, we lashed the helm down to leeward and hove *Loon* to.

I was amazed, as always, by the sense of peace that came after heaving-to. The seas were still big, and occasionally one slopped aboard, but *Loon* was reaching slowly ahead at about one knot, making about a half knot of leeway, and her motion had eased tremendously. It seemed almost as peaceful as being at anchor in a protected harbor. We had supper, and, since Briggs Tobin and Sally had very kindly offered to alternate standing "anchor watch," the rest of us crawled rejoicingly into the sack.

Later that night, Sally woke me up to tell me that a steamer was bearing down on us on what looked like a collision course, and she couldn't raise them on the radio. I got out the big Very pistol with a white flare, went up on deck and shot it off with a very satisfactory roar. This gave me a good feeling of having done something positive, but unfortunately it didn't solve our problem, since it failed to ignite. We next turned on the masthead strobe light, and the steamer immediately put a spotlight on us and turned away to miss us by a reasonable distance. Masthead strobes may be illegal, except in an emergency, but they are worth their weight in gold in alerting steamers to your presence. Twice that summer we had the experience of a ship bearing down on us, apparently unaware of our existence until we turned on the strobe.

There's an old saying that the first fifty years are the hardest. For Sally and me, looking back after more than fifty years of sailing, they were wonderful, romantic, exciting, and superb fun. With them behind us, an ordinary summer gale is something to be treated with respect, but it doesn't have to be worn as a hair shirt. When you're not racing, there's no reason not to heave to and enjoy it, rather than pressing on to show how tough you are. Accidents happen to tired crews, and the best ones avoid fatigue when they can. I think that doing just that has helped to keep our sailing happy for all these years.

This book is the story of the first twenty-nine years we sailed together. We had such a good time that I thought other people might be interested in how we learned to cruise and race and would enjoy hearing about the fascinating, often exotic people who became our friends along the way. Finally, since there's more to be had from cruising and racing than just sailing, I've included some of the science and natural history that made the places we visited even more fascinating to us. It's about what it was like to sail and race without the electronic aids that everyone relies on and takes for granted nowadays. There was no Loran or radar when we began—no Fathometers or speedometers. Sailors were quite happy with a compass, a patent log, a sextant, and a lead line, plus a very carefully kept record of courses and distances sailed. We didn't need electronic wind indicators to tell us where the wind was from—we used the masthead pennant and the hairs on the backs of our necks. We learned to tell whether the boat was at maximum speed by feel, without gauges and computers; nor did fog and bad weather keep us in harbor any more than they do now, when we have more instruments. We chose to do without an engine for twenty-four years, which made the whole thing much more fun and gave us a feeling of achievement and independence that you just don't have if you can start the engine whenever the breeze drops or comes ahead. Sailing without these crutches put skill at a premium. Perhaps there was more risk, but feeling our way under sail in thick fog to a friendly and welcoming harbor gave us a thrill that doesn't come after motoring in using Loran. And when, inevitably, the Loran misbehaves or the engine quits, we can, and do, go happily ahead without them, just as we always did.

Loki and Loon

1

A passion for boats and the sea started for Sally and me a long time ago. We began our seagoing lives in very different ways. She sailed as crew for her father, George Richards (later commodore of the Cruising Club of America) on a Crosby Cat, and later in the Colin Archer-type cruising ketch *Freya*. She also sailed and raced a variety of daysailers for almost as long as she can remember. When I met her, she and her sister had their own gaff-rigged Indian class sloop, *Sowama,* which Sally raced at the Norwalk Yacht Club.

Sally's father was one of the most universally loved and respected men I have ever known, a fine sailor, and an excellent teacher. *Freya* may not have been very fast (which never kept him from trying to beat every other boat he saw), but everyone who sailed on *Freya* loved her; she produced a wonderful sense of warmth and homeyness, a quality that is lacking in many faster, more modern boats. Sally couldn't have had a better beginning for her cruising life.

My nautical upbringing was quite different. I grew up inland, but my father loved canoes and fishing out of them, and gave me one of my own as soon as I proved that I could swim the length of the pond where it was to be used. I was about six at the time. I spent many happy times fishing with him in canoes after that.

Ever since college, my father had wanted to take a cruise to the South Pacific, even though he was not really a sailor. After a long search up and down the whole Eastern Seaboard for exactly the right boat, he bought a 150-foot schooner for this voyage. He outfitted her in Brooklyn, rechristened her the *Mary Pinchot* after his mother, and in the spring of 1929, when I was thirteen years old, I was taken out of boarding school for an eight-and-a-half-month cruise through the Caribbean and the Panama Canal to the

Galápagos, then across three thousand miles of the Pacific to the Marquesas. From there we sailed to the Tuomotus, and finally ended up in Tahiti. I can't imagine anything more exciting and wonderful for a thirteen-year-old than this sort of an adventure. My family asked my best friend Steve "Stiff" Stahlnecker to come along, so I had someone of my own age to have fun with as well as the whole ship's crew of sixteen men. My particular friend in the crew was the second mate, Les Bourget, who came from Port-

Freya

land, Maine. He was a fine seaman and spent many hours teaching me to sew sails and make ditty bags and sail bags, as well as how to whip and splice rope, and varnish—an almost continuous job on a big yacht in the tropics. He impressed on me the great importance of keeping my sheath knife "shaving sharp." Les ran the ship's launch, and I spent a lot of time in it, as I was doing most of the handline fishing to supply the galley. The *Mary* also had a ship's lifeboat with a sailing rig in it, and it was in this that I spent many happy hours learning to sail in some of the world's loveliest harbors.

Strange and romantic islands in the Caribbean; the Panama Canal; Cocos Island with its reputed buried treasure, incredible fishing, and marine life; the moonlike, barren landscapes of the Galápagos with "wild" animals largely unafraid of men; the tortoises, iguanas, the sea lions we swam with—all left a fantastic impression. The Marquesas, with their high mountains cut in steep valleys running to the sea and covered with greenery, and the contrasting low, sandy islands of the Tuomotus, with their fringe of palm trees—I can still see them now, more than fifty years later. We did our first diving in the Tuomotus, wearing copper helmets with lead weights to hold them on our shoulders, supplied with air from a hand pump in a boat on the surface. This was my introduction to the extraordinarily beautiful underwater world of coral and of fantastically colored fish that swam around us without fear.

We came home from Tahiti by steamer to San Francisco. On the way back to the East Coast by train, we stopped at the Grand Canyon. My father had packed in there on horseback long before it was a tourist attraction, and was quite annoyed with me because I wasn't more impressed by it. After what I had seen in the South Pacific, it just didn't seem very exciting!

The cruise on the *Mary Pinchot* had a profound effect on my life. I had been brought up with the very strong feeling, which sounds very dated and almost ridiculous nowadays, that you should try your very best to do something useful with your life; to put it baldly, to try to leave the world a better place than you found it.

My father did, I think, achieve just that, as a leading figure in the conservation movement, especially in Theodore Roosevelt's time, when he started the U.S. Forest Service and popularized the need for conservation and natural resource management. Stiff and I became interested in medicine through the ship's doctor, and we both ended up going to medical school—he practiced, and I went into research.

On the other hand, the trip gave me a taste for adventure that made it very difficult to be satisfied in a life without it. My father must have had the same problem, since he often quoted to me the statement that man's highest duty was to undertake adventure. Now a taste for excitement, and the financial ability to satisfy it, isn't an ideal prerequisite for a scientific career—it doesn't make it easy to settle down to research, which can be very boring in the day-to-day routine. But if you give in to your desire for adventure, your colleagues can't help regarding you as a playboy. The South Seas cruise had complex aftereffects. I might have been a better scientist without that experience, or at least worked more hours, but it did introduce me to one of the great joys of my life. From then on I was completely convinced that there was nothing more wonderful than sailing your own boat to foreign ports. Boats and the sea came to mean the ultimate in romance and adventure to me on that cruise, and they still do. I have never been sorry that I went.

A few years later, when I was a freshman in college, I met Sally Richards at a dance in Wilton, Connecticut. Not too long after that she took me sailing on her sloop, and I regaled her at great length with the story of how one of the scientists on the *Mary Pinchot* had plugged up the marine toilet that I shared with him by trying to flush peanut shells through it, and then blamed it on me. I guess I had a pretty strange idea of small talk.

It was quite obvious to me from the beginning that Sally was the girl I wanted to marry. She was extremely attractive, she was self-confident, and she was good at everything she did. She rode a horse like an angel and was an excellent sailor. She also loved adventure and felt a great obligation to do something significant

Learning to sail in the Marquesas (PHOTO BY HOWARD CLEAVES)

The Mary Pinchot

with her life. There was only one drawback—she was a year older than I was, and wasn't at all sure that a mere child of eighteen was what she wanted for a husband. I managed to wear her down over the next couple of years (and flunked a course in college in the process), and it was apparent that if we were going to get married, what we really needed was a boat.

My mother knew the famous sailor Paul Hammond and asked him for advice about how I should go about finding a boat for Sally and me. He suggested that he was about to sell his schooner *Niña* for $12,500, and that she was just what we needed. At 59 feet long and that price, she seemed a bit big and expensive, so Paul suggested that we try the then almost brand-new firm of brokers and designers called Sparkman & Stephens. This was good advice indeed. At their offices, I met Bob Garland, and he produced particulars and pictures of a lot of boats, most of which were bigger and fancier than we wanted or could afford. Then I saw a model of a beautiful sloop in a glass case in his office. She had a very tall rig and very pretty underwater lines. She turned out to be a Kretzer 30, of which eight were built by Will and Clarence Kretzer at their yard in City Island, New York. They were trial horses for the famous New York 32s, which were built at Nevins Yard a year or two later. The lines were similar, but the New York 32s were 32 feet on the waterline and 45 feet overall, while the Kretzer boats were 30 feet overall and 22′4″ on the water, with a beam of 8′2″ and a draft of 4′4″. They had a main hoist of 37 feet, making for fine light-weather performance, with a long forefoot, so they tacked quickly and handled beautifully. They were close-winded and fast, and were real thoroughbreds. Down below they were quite simple, with a transverse seat forward of the mast that opened up to reveal a head. Aft of this, there were two settees too narrow to sleep on, with folding pipe berths above them. Still farther aft, there was a galley on one side and a hanging locker on the other. A Gray four-cylinder engine lived under the companionway stairs and cockpit. We found to our delight that one of these lovely boats was available for $3,000, complete with sails and an engine, and she was only eight months old.

I had some money that I'd made writing a book—*Giff and Stiff in the South Seas*—so it wasn't long after we saw her that I bought our first boat. We changed her name to *Nankipoo* because Sally was singing that year in the Blue Hill Troop's production of *The Mikado*. Early in May, Sally and her mother, father, brother Fred, and I went to City Island to pick her up. There was a nice breeze, and we swung her off the mooring under sail and headed out by Execution Rock and eastward up the Sound. The breeze soon died, and when I tried to start the engine, it refused to go. The gas tank was empty. I ended up in the dink, towing *Nankipoo* into Indian

Harbor and leaving her there for the night. Sally and her family took it all in good spirits, but my face was pretty red. This was not the way I had hoped to impress my future father-in-law with my nautical skill.

Sally's father wrote up the log for this part of the sail as follows:

> 1325 Passed Execution Bearing NW x N $^{1}/_{4}$ Mile
> Lunch
> 1435 Passed Matinecock
> Wind East
> Soon Wind 0
> Rain
> Rowed for Greenwich
> Fog
> Picked Up Buoys and a little East wind
> Sailed to Y.C., Moored
> Dinner, 19th Hole, Dodge Home.

As I look back over the log of our honeymoon cruise and the minor but embarrassing disasters it so carefully understates, I wonder that Sally and I continued to cruise together or even stayed married to each other. We had a major problem that I don't think either of us quite recognized at the time. It is now clear that Sally had a lot more experience with this sort of cruising in small boats than I did, but obviously, in that era, as the man I was going to have to be the skipper. Even more important was the fact that while we had both cruised a good deal, neither of us had ever had the experience of being in charge of a cruising boat. It takes a lot more know-how to make the right decisions than to carry out someone else's. We both had a great deal to learn, as we very soon found out.

The day after we were married that June, we drove to Norwalk and loaded *Nankipoo* for our first cruise. We had a fine sail with a lovely northerly breeze from Norwalk to Morris Cove inside the New Haven breakwater. We anchored but found we were slowly dragging the small kedge, so I got the fifty-pounder from below and made it up to its rode. We were anxious to do everything under sail, so I set the main and got up the small anchor, and Sally let the boat fall off to sail up the harbor. This maneuver brought us closer than we wanted to be to the boat behind us, but *Nanki*, always a lady, heeled over and started to sail. Shortly after this, both anchors slid overboard. We were lucky enough not to lose both rodes, even though, at this stage in our career, the bitter ends probably weren't made fast to anything. Eventually I was able to get both anchors back on deck without falling overboard myself, and we anchored again. This time the big kedge held. So far no damage to anything but our egos, but they were a bit bruised.

The next day, we had a fine breeze, which took us to an anchorage in Duck Island Roads. On the way, we were passed by a Herreshoff Buzzards Bay 30, the *West Wind*. As she passed us, her owners asked us aboard for a drink in Duck Island, and when we got there, we had a delightful time with them. How much more friendly cruising was in those days, when you just assumed that anyone in a sailboat would be congenial company for an evening get-together.

The following day's excitement was that the bell buoy on the east end of Long Sand Shoal was missing, and I was in a state, for fear of going over the shoal and going aground. I completely ignored the fact that *Nankipoo* drew only a little over four feet, and the shoal at that end is well over ten feet deep.

Where I had learned to sail, in my father's schooner, which drew sixteen feet, groundings were serious business. Her first professional skipper put her aground three times between New York and Panama. His replacement grounded her again on Barrington Island in the Galápagos, which could have been quite unpleasant. It happened at night when this skipper was trying to take her off the anchor under sail, and she fell away on the wrong tack. Instead of simply anchoring again and getting her off on the right tack, he rang down for full astern on the engine and ultimately backed her into the lava island itself, bending her rudder post and steering gear so that the rudder could only be turned from amidships to port. Thanks to the quick thinking of my friend, the second mate, we put the launch overboard and towed her head to starboard, got her out of the harbor and anchored outside. The next day, we dismantled the gear and rigged a jury tiller on top of the rudder post, and fortunately were able to sail her back to Panama for repairs, all the way on starboard tack. This episode on an uninhabited island, which had no fresh water, plus the three other groundings earlier in the cruise, made me a good deal more shy of the bottom than I needed to be in *Nankipoo*—at least until I discovered that, in light groundings, I could stand on the bottom and get my shoulder under her counter and push her off.

Just before we got to the east end of Long Sand Shoal that day, a Coast Guard tender came and put the buoy down just where we expected it to be, which was a great relief to me. Later that afternoon, we met Sally's mother and father on *Freya* at Burr's Landing in New London and went ashore for dinner with them. This was the beginning of many years of joint cruising with the Richardses and being royally entertained in *Freya*'s cozy cabin after a day of sailing on our own boat. Sailing on two boats is an ideal way for different generations to cruise together. The young learners have their privacy and all the fun of being on their own and making their own mistakes during the day, but in the evenings are also in contact with more experienced sailors from whom they can learn a great deal. At the end of a long, cold day, a drink in *Freya*'s cabin, warmed by her coal Shipmate stove, enjoying good conversation with the Richardses, was always a delight.

We were gradually getting things organized on *Nankipoo,* and the log says we sent our suitcases home from New London. How very unsophisticated we were, not to know that hard suitcases were completely out of place on a small cruising boat. There were no adequate lockers for clothes on *Nankipoo*, but we developed a fine method for handling the problem. We kept our clothes in two sausage bags with full-length zippers. The bags were folded up in the pipe berths during the day and put on the settees under the bunks at night. The cabin stayed neat, and the clothes were always available. Above each bunk, we hung a net to keep small things in, like those on Pullman cars (for those who can remember such things). We solved the chart stowage problem by hanging them rolled, printed side out, from the cast bronze knees connecting the sides with the top of the house. At the beginning of the cruise, all the charts were on one roll, with the chart of Norwalk outside. When we finished with a chart, we shifted it to a second roll, which got fatter with charts as we sailed eastward, until we turned west again and reversed the process. This made finding charts easy (except for side trips like going out to Nantucket) and helped to keep the cabin neat.

We built a table with three leaves that folded up around the square mast when not in use, but came down with a hinged leg on the cabin sole when we wanted it. This we used to eat on and as a chart table. Charts rolled printed side out were easy to use, since the ends curled around the table top and held the charts in place.

Nankipoo had a pot locker under the stove, a drawer for silver, and a rack for plates. Usually things stayed pretty much in place, but I do remember one noisy night before dinner when Sally was a bit piqued about something and couldn't find one particular pot. She had them all out on the cabin sole and was trying to locate the one she wanted by sorting through them with her feet. She now stoutly denies this. At any rate, we quickly discovered that good storage systems helped prevent total chaos when we were sailing.

More embarrassments that first summer were not long in coming. Sailing out from Newport to see the beginning of the Bermuda Race, we came close to being run down by *Sea Dream,* a big square-rigger under power, because we weren't sure whether her two blasts on the horn meant "leave me to starboard" or "leave me to port." The log says "the former won, but not by much." Later that day, going into Cuttyhunk Harbor in a good breeze, we found the buoys all rusted to the same dingy red color. This produced another flap until we realized that we could tell nuns and cans apart by their shape, and so got things figured out.

In Woods Hole, we sailed to the Penzance Dock to load food and get the tail-shaft packing nut tightened to stop a minor leak.

Nankipoo, *York Harbor, Maine*

By the time we were ready to go, the breeze was in hard, blowing us against the dock. Sally's comments in the log follow.

> Now it was all we could do to hold her off. Started the motor and got clear of the dock, then Sally insisted on trying to sail out. Mess of lines on deck aided confusion and strong currents setting on dock completed it. Got sail up, but not in time to get enough headway to come about against the current. Giff held her off the dock, but had to let the main

> sheet go. Engine started and in reverse, nearly rammed fisherman. With his help we got clear. Giff got the mainsail down and we motored out into comparative safety and back to Great Harbor, where we picked up mooring.

I can still feel the agonies of embarrassment hidden by those words!

Sally's father later gave us an invaluable piece of advice to help avoid such mistakes as this. He said: Plan your maneuver in detail before you start, then assume it goes wrong and plan your recovery. It is a first-rate precept. I wish I had always followed it.

The next day, we had a fine sail to Nantucket after gorging on a breakfast of omelette and cornbread. This was our first sail out of sight of land, and we were very pleased with ourselves.

We finally brought *Nankipoo* home to her mooring at Norwalk. I had a college course to make up in summer school, partly as a result of spending almost more time visiting Sally at Vassar than I did studying at Yale. In spite of all our ineptitudes, we knew we loved cruising. Even though I was officially skipper, it was very much a joint operation. We had individual jobs, of course, but we were determined to work things out together. We're still doing it forty-five years later, and there is no one I can rely on as completely and work with as happily as Sally.

2

For our second year's cruise, Sally suggested that it might be more fun if we took the engine out and left it ashore. This we did, and to replace it we bought a twelve-foot oar, which we carried on deck. To row, we used a stanchion amidships on the starboard side as an oarlock and lashed the oar to it. One person rowed and the other steered. Surprisingly, once we got *Nankipoo* moving, it took almost no rudder to keep her going straight.

Having no engine, we couldn't help learning the fine points of sailing much more quickly than we would have with power to fall back on in light airs or difficult situations. We became much more conscious of optimal sail trim all the time, rather than just when we were racing. Each time we had to buck the tide around a headland or sail through Woods Hole against the current, we had to concentrate on getting the most out of the boat. We learned how to get in and out of tight places, making downwind docks and getting off them, too.

One of the great delights of having no power is seeing and feeling the breeze come in after you have been becalmed. Little ripples appear on the glassy surface and quietly, almost imperceptibly, the boat begins to move, and the frustration of sitting still is replaced by the joy of sailing. If you have an engine you miss this completely, since you resort to power when the wind drops and start charging along noisily at six knots. You're not aware of the wind when it first comes back, and even if you finally admit to yourself that there is wind enough to sail, there is no thrill in stopping the engine and then poking along at two or three knots. On the other hand, after standing still for several hours, slipping silently along at two or three knots becomes pure heaven.

That first summer without an engine, Sally wrote in the log, "Both decided that having the engine out makes everything much more fun, though we can't quite understand why." It was more fun, I think, because we were on our own with no artificial aids. It made our senses sharper, our insurance cheaper, and completely eliminated arguments about whether or not to start the engine.

We continued without power for the next twenty-four years, and surprisingly, in all this time, the lack of an engine only once made me late for work. Even if we were becalmed around sunset, there was usually a light offshore breeze during the night, and using this, or sometimes the big oar, or by towing with the dinghy, we never failed to get in sometime. I must admit we have picked up the mooring at seven or eight in the morning and gone to work at nine a few times, but this isn't a bad trade for getting rid of the smell and bother of an engine.

We learned our sailing before most of the modern electronic navigation aids were available to small cruising boats. Many, such as Loran and radar, hadn't even been invented. Just as we learned the fine points of sailing without an engine, so we had to learn the basics of navigation without electronics. We learned to rely on all sorts of hints that you wouldn't think of using if you had Loran and radar (we still don't have radar and only got Loran in 1984)—such hints in the fog as the decrease in waves in the lee of an island, or the confused wave reflection pattern from a nearby bold shore. The sound or smell of gulls on a beach or of shorebirds on an island can also be very useful in telling where you are. You can estimate your distance from a high shore by timing how long an echo takes to return. Sound travels a nautical mile in 5.5 seconds. It has to go both ways, so an echo returns from land a mile away in 11 seconds. These tricks may prove to be worth their weight in gold if you have fancy electronics that stop working at a critical moment in the fog, as they sometimes do.

In June of the second year we had *Nankipoo,* we were about to enter her in her first race, the third annual Duck Island Race, run by the Norwalk Yacht Club. The first leg was about forty nautical miles, from Norwalk to Duck Island with an overnight stay there, and a return the next day. There were two classes for boats with engines and one, Class C, for those of us with no power.

The race started on the morning of June 11, just three days after we got *Nankipoo* out of the yard. We didn't have a spinnaker or a genoa, but a member of the Norwalk Yacht Club very kindly lent us a flat spinnaker for the race. We liked it so much we bought it from him later for ten dollars. Today it would be hard to buy a grommet for that kind of money.

There were all sorts of last-minute jobs to be done, such as getting the twelve-foot sweep from New York and a code flag "N" to be flown during the race. The compass had to be checked, stores bought and brought aboard, charts gone over, and all the myriad details taken care of that appear on the "To Do" list before a race. Even this "busy work" was new and exciting then.

The crew consisted of Sally, her sister Minnie, and Minnie's husband Max. The watches were divided up so that the men were on one and the ladies on the other. The start was in almost flat calm, but a gentle westerly sprang up shortly after we set the "new" spinnaker, and we seemed to be doing well with the other non-auxiliaries in our class. The off-watch did complain of trouble sleeping, as the watch on deck kept tramping around setting, trimming, handing, and then resetting the spinnaker to suit the fitful breeze.

During one of the sail changes that night, the spinnaker refused to come down. I went aloft on the jib halyard, sitting in a bosun's chair, to find out what was wrong. When I arrived, I couldn't reach the trouble and had to stand up on the chair. The tongue snap hook, which in my ignorance I had used on the spinnaker halyard, had snapped itself around the jumper stay above the strut and effectively locked the spinnaker aloft. To free it, I unsnapped the spinnaker from the halyard. Then, holding the sail in my left hand and ignoring the old rule of one hand for the ship and one for yourself, I unsnapped the halyard from the stay with my right. All this was done balanced standing up in the chair. After this it was simple to reattach the halyard to the sail and come back down on deck. I was very glad to arrive, and was more than grateful that there had been almost no wind or left-over sea during this maneuver. On deck I lowered the sail and replaced the snap hook with a knot before rehoisting it. It goes without saying that we never used tongue snap hooks on halyards again.

We got into Duck Island by midafternoon the next day, which happened to be our first wedding anniversary. *Freya* was there already with the orchids that I'd bought for Sally before the race started. After supper, we took *Freya*'s crew for a sail around the harbor on *Nankipoo,* and Mr. Richards showed us a trick for making a controlled shoot in a cramped space. He "sailed" the downwind leg with no jib and the mainsail furled, but with the boom swung way out to give the boat just a little way. The object is to go so slowly that after two 90-degree turns to head the boat upwind, she is almost completely stopped. This makes it easy to estimate exactly where the boat will end up, since she doesn't shoot far after the upwind turn. *Nankipoo,* with her long, sloping forefoot, didn't use up a lot of energy in a 180-degree turn. In a boat with a longer keel, you can leave up a little mainsail to insure that she doesn't stop before the second turn is completed. We've used this trick many times, and it works beautifully.

The race home the next day started in a flat calm. As the westerly breeze came in, boats were spread all over the Sound, so it was hard to tell how we were doing. After the finish, we were very pleased to find that we'd ended up third in our class of six. Not too disgraceful for our first race on *Nankipoo,* with a borrowed spinnaker and no genoa!

This was the kind of life we lived in *Nankipoo*—an occasional race, and some joint cruising with *Freya* or on our own. One memorable year, with Mr. Richards' great friend Rob Keep, who had chartered the 55-foot Alden Schooner *Lord Jim,* we had a joint cruise of three boats. *Nankipoo* was so handy under sail that we sometimes acted as a launch for the bigger boats.

Sailing with *Freya,* we learned another useful trick for getting off a dock with wind blowing hard on it. This was the same situation and the same dock that had left us with such red faces the year before. *Freya* and *Nankipoo* were both at the Penzance Dock with the wind blowing directly onto it. Sally's father showed us that if we got as much way on as possible, by pushing her along the dock, we could shoot out beyond it, round up, and get the main on before losing way. This way, we could sail off the dock rather than tow her out with a dinghy. It worked so well for us that he did the same maneuver successfully with *Freya* a few minutes later. This took more doing, since *Freya* was not as easy to push as *Nankipoo* and not as quick to pick up way under sail.

Our self-confidence was slowly growing. Sally said in the log that year: "Giff shot a solo mooring beautifully, only to find it wasn't ours. Missed ours out of laziness, and finally got it on the second try. We didn't even care. What a contrast to last year when we would have been covered with shame at such an occurrence."

We gradually updated our sail inventory, buying a parachute spinnaker and a genoa jib, after consulting Rod Stephens about their design and cutting down *Nanki*'s spreaders so that the genoa could be properly sheeted. When we first met Rod, he and his brother Olin were already the leading designers of racing sailboats in this country, and perhaps in the world. Olin drew the lines, and Rod took care of the rigging, accommodations, and inspection of the boats as they were built. Rod had worked his way through all the departments of the most famous yacht-building yard in the country, Nevins at City Island, so he had a very thorough knowledge of building as well as sailing ocean racers. He had already skippered and won two transatlantic races, and two Fastnet Races in England with Olin's and his yawl *Dorade* and Phillip LeBoutillier's *Stormy Weather*. Their designs had won Bermuda Races and been class winners even more often. Olin had also been involved in the design of the famous *Ranger,* last of the J-boats, and sailed in her afterguard when she defended the *America*'s Cup in 1937. Rod was in charge of the rigging and foredeck in that campaign. He had won the highest sailing award in this country, the Blue Water Medal of the Cruising Club of America. In spite of all his fame, he was modest and more than willing to help anyone who asked his advice. It is no wonder that he was the model that most of us tried to emulate. I quoted him so often that one of my crew christened him "Rod-God."

I finally finished college and was admitted to the College of

Physicians and Surgeons (P & S) in New York. After our second year of cruising in *Nankipoo,* we rented an apartment in Riverdale and layed *Nankipoo* up at Kretzer's in City Island, where she had been built. Will Kretzer, who can't have been over five feet tall, was a determined and outspoken person, but he seemed to be glad to have her back. Our discussion about what had to be done on her was carried out down below. Sally and I had to bend over or sit down to keep from hitting our heads on the cabin top (*Nanki* had about five feet of headroom), but Will, with his thumbs hooked under his suspenders, strode up and down the minuscule cabin, often venting his irritation with Rod Stephens, since they both had firm ideas about how things should be done and didn't always agree.

We hauled *Nanki* early in September. I went to medical school while Sally handled the move into our new apartment. It poured with rain, which didn't make the move any easier, and I was impressed by how windy it was around P & S and wondered if it always blew this hard in the Bronx. Neither of us realized at the time that we had chosen to move on the day of a hurricane, the notorious one of 1938, in which so many people were killed and so many boats were wrecked.

Fortunately ours was not among them. Will Kretzer lashed his boats into their cradles as the tide rose so that when the water went out again, they wouldn't fall over on their sides, as so many boats from other yards did. The main street of City Island had boats lying in it after the tide went out. Since *Nanki* had no engine and since we'd taken everything out of her, Will left the plug out of her bottom so that she filled and sank in her cradle and didn't move. The only damage she suffered showed up the next summer when we tried to light the kerosene sidelights and found them full of water.

Will Kretzer could be ill-tempered if he didn't like you. I remember his disgust with inspectors during the war, when he was building wooden boats for the government. The inspectors, he said, were a bunch of "farmers," and the only paint he could get wasn't paint at all, it was "goddamned onion juice." The only time I ever saw Will make a mistake was one afternoon after we'd hauled *Nanki* on his very steep railway and were just about to put her back into the water on a falling tide. He was in a hurry to get her in before the tide went out so far that she wouldn't float, and was just about to let her go when the buzzer rang for a phone call. Will hooked a chain to the cradle in case the winch slipped. When he came back from the phone call, he'd forgotten about the chain, and so had I. He let the winch go with a run. *Nanki* and I were picking up speed fast on the steep railway when we came to the end of the chain. The cradle stopped, but the boat and I didn't. I was just trying to make up my mind whether to jump into the water about fifteen feet below or to try for the dock on the other side, when I realized that *Nanki* had stopped too, and was still upright in the cradle. She'd slid back two or three feet, but was otherwise intact. Will unhooked the chain and let her go with a run again, and she didn't quite ground out. Neither of us ever referred to this incident later.

After a winter at med school working as I had never worked before, we had an almost four-month summer vacation to look forward to. The summer of '39 was one of fog, fog, and more fog. The log says we found Portuguese men-of-war in Buzzards Bay, so the Gulf Stream must have come in very close to shore. Toward the end of July, Sally and I started east one evening. After an all-night sail, we picked up a friend at Stonington and kept going. That evening the fog came in solid, and by the time we were near the Hen and Chickens lightship at about midnight, the fog was a real pea-souper, the wind was just about nonexistent, and we had almost no steerageway. While the navigation was easy with all the fog signals along that coast, there was one other problem. We weren't the only ones using the lightship as a turning mark. This was long before radar, and our only defense was a mouth-blown foghorn, since it was also before the days of Freon foghorns or even the "supertoots" that we had after the war, which were made up of a diaphragm horn hooked to an oversized tire pump. So we sat becalmed for hours that night, blowing our guts out on the foghorn as big ships passed uncomfortably close by. Once we actually looked up into the lighted wheelhouse of a tug as it passed a few feet away. By this time we were good and scared, and finally got out the twelve-foot oar and rowed out of the shipping lane over toward the Old Cock reef. With dawn, a little breeze came up, and after listening carefully for steamers, we crossed the shipping lane at the lightship and took up a course to Cuttyhunk Pond, which we found in the fog without any trouble. What a relief it was to sail in and get the hook down in such a protected spot! We anchored at eight-thirty in the morning and all went to sleep until five-thirty that afternoon, when hunger finally woke us up.

Radar has simplified fog navigation for those who have it, and also made it safer for those who don't, since even the small commercial ships have it and are a little less likely to run you down, if you use a radar reflector. On the other hand, fog navigation without radar is a bit harder than it used to be. In the thirties and forties, there were many different kinds of foghorns—diaphones, reed horns, diaphragm horns, sirens, and even fog guns in Nova Scotia. Each made a distinctive sound so that it could be easily recognized. Foghorns were also generally lower-pitched in those days, and the lower the pitch, the easier it is to distinguish direction. Nowadays, they are almost all of the identical high-pitched horn variety, and it is much harder, if not impossible, to get an accurate bearing from them. They are also much weaker than they used to be and can't be heard from as far away. Furthermore, a buoy or a fog signal is of no use unless you can identify it and know exactly where it is. The current idiotic bureaucratic practice of changing everything periodically probably makes an administrator feel that he is accomplishing something, but it very much confuses the issue for those of us who are using the navigational aids.

In sailing east that year in *Nankipoo,* we needed a tow through the Cape Cod Canal, since it is against the law to go through without power. We had a fair wind and a head tide and wanted to stop at the Corps of Engineers dock at the west end of the canal to arrange a tow. We used another trick that Sally's father had shown us for making a dock under these conditions. In essence, we lowered all but just enough sail to buck the current and moved very slowly toward our destination, so that we arrived under complete control, allowing me to step onto the float and tie *Nanki* up with ease.

We got a tow through the canal for ten dollars and sailed as far east as Marblehead, then came home slowly with day after day of light winds and fog. When we were becalmed during the daytime, we read aloud to each other, or swam, or caught up with odd jobs around the boat. There was time to go on picnics with friends out of Woods Hole, to joint cruise with *Freya,* and to have an occasional race. It was a very relaxed and pleasant summer without any fixed schedule.

In 1940 a long cruise was out of the question because Sally and I were starting a family. But we did get as far as the Vineyard in a short and lazy summer. It seemed very wrong to sail to City Island in September to lay the boat up, with Sally left standing on the dock, by doctor's orders, as we sailed away. A couple of weeks later, Marianna, named after her grandmother Richards, made her appearance to the delight of all. In fact, Sally's mother was so pleased, that she was more than willing to keep young Marianna while we went sailing the next summer. I think she probably believed that she was doing a much better job of bringing her up than we could, and maybe she was right. She continued this much-appreciated project when our two sons Sandy and Peter made their subsequent appearances, so we were able to continue cruising together while the children were too small to come with us.

The summer of '41 was the last chance for a real cruise before the war shut things down for good. Sally's mother and father had rented a cottage for part of the summer at Woods Hole, so our base was there. In addition to *Nankipoo,* we had a Polynesian outrigger canoe from the island of Raiatea with us in Woods Hole that summer. This had been a present to me from Charles Nordhoff of *Mutiny on the Bounty* fame. My father had given him an Old Town canoe when we were in Tahiti in 1929, and he had kindly responded by sending this fascinating boat. The bottom of the hull was hollowed out of a single tree trunk, with one strake of planking above it sewed to the log and to adjoining planks with sennet (braided coconut fiber). The boat was twenty-four feet long and eighteen inches wide outside the gunwale. It was great fun to sail—very fast on one tack, when you could lift the outrigger log out of water on the windward side. One of these canoes was reputedly clocked at twenty-five knots in Raiatea. Tacking was another matter, though, since it steered with an enormous paddle that must have weighed seventy-five pounds. The canoe lost way as we brought it upwind, and we had to paddle it around the rest of the way. If you weren't careful, you could get going backward very fast when in irons. This boat is now in the Peabody Museum in Salem, Massachusetts.

We did some more racing that year, entering *Nankipoo* in the Edgartown Regatta. On our first day's race, we missed seeing a reverse-course signal and, along with about half the fleet, sailed the course the wrong way around. We did better the next day in the overnight race around the Vineyard, ending up with a second in our class.

Raiatea canoe, Woods Hole, Massachusetts

Later that year, Sally and I took off alone for a cruise to Maine. We started sailing through the Cape Cod Canal, illegally this time, with a good breeze, and were offered a tow about two-thirds of the way through, which got us safely by the officials at the east end of the canal. We had a delightful overnight sail to Maine and eventually got as far east as Tenants Harbor.

We used a fresh northerly to head home, making Marblehead in twenty hours, then worked our way back by harbor-hopping. Later that fall, we layed *Nanki* up at Kretzer's Yard again, and this turned out to be our last real cruise aboard her. We sold her before the war ended, which certainly was a mistake, as we could have gotten a lot more for her after peace was declared.

3

The war was finally won, and my active duty in the navy, doing research at Camp Detrick, Maryland, ended in the summer of 1946. I found a research job and later a teaching job at the Yale medical school, and with this under control, we began thinking about a boat to replace *Nankipoo.* We looked at some secondhand boats, but none of them seemed to fill the bill, so we went to see Olin and Rod Stephens about having a new one built. We told them we wanted a yawl of 35 to 40 feet overall, with no engine. She had to be beautiful, fast, and able to take us on longer voyages, perhaps even as far as the Caribbean. Olin listened and didn't say much, but thought that 38 feet, which we finally decided on, was too small for a yawl, so the first two sets of drawings showed a very pretty sloop with an engine. Finally, after a number of conferences, we got plans for a really beautiful 38-foot yawl without an engine, which we later named *Loki,* after the Norse god of fire and mischief. Olin had the last word, however, because after she was built, the plans came out in *Rudder.* The designer's comment included the statement that "in his opinion, she was too small to be rigged as a yawl." This didn't stop the firm later from building a series of twelve boats in Germany to the same plans, called the "Loki Yawls." In our eyes, the yawl rig was ideal, since with only two of us on board, it was so easy to drop the main for a blow, rather than reefing. *Loki* handled beautifully under jib and jigger, and the mizzen staysail was not measured at this time under the handicap rule, and was therefore an added bonus for a racing yawl.

Once we had the plans and an estimated price from several good yards, we agonized about whether or not we could afford her. This was really an exercise in futility, since there was no way short of starvation that we weren't going to scrape up the money to have her built. Rod Stephens then suggested Albert Lemos of Riverside, Rhode Island, as less expensive than the fancy yards in City Island, but still a first-class builder. We took Rod's advice without any hesitation.

About every two weeks during that winter (1947 to 1948), Rod appeared, and we drove from New Haven to Riverside, Rhode Island, to see what progress had been made. What an exciting winter that was for us, seeing *Loki* come to life. The smells of wood shavings and cuprinol still bring back the wonderful memories of her building and the skills of the men working on her.

Albert Lemos had been born in the Azores. He was an extremely dignified, white-haired gentleman who, from his looks, might well have been a professor of philosophy at Harvard. In fact, he had never learned to read easily. With him were two more Portuguese shipwrights who had worked at Herreshoff's for years before that yard was finally shut down. They had been trained never to look up at visitors unless they were spoken to. It was very impressive to see one of them cutting out the rabbit in the stem with a one-handed adze, taking off a precise shaving of a sixty-fourth of an inch at each controlled stroke. We were fascinated by the whole procedure and by Rod's clear and concise explanation of every step in the process.

There were always things for us to decide. On one occasion, it was the precise placement and height of the toilet in the head. Rod, always a realist, suggested that we block it up temporarily and try it out. So we all did, with dry runs, much to Albert's embarrassment. Anyway, this committee decision, unlike so many, turned out to be just right.

Finally, the great day came in April for the launching. *Loki* looked absolutely perfect in her Endeavor Blue paint, white boot top, red bottom paint, and the signal flags. Albert had dressed her in. With everyone watching, Sally stepped up on a box underneath the bow with a bottle of champagne and took a mighty swing. The bottle broke, the fizz fizzed, and Sally followed through and fell off the box. Rod had so impressed her with the horrors of not

Loki *ready for launching*

breaking the bottle that she had given it her all, which turned out to be a lot more than was needed. Worse was yet to come. It was blowing hard from the north, and the wind had lowered the water level a couple of feet below the expected high tide. *Loki* got out to the end of the railway and refused to float. Oh well, she did float very well the next day, and exactly on her lines. Albert and his crew had done a superb job.

Loki was towed down to Warren, Rhode Island, for final fitting-out. Sally and I, with Rod and Albert's son Bill (later a full admiral in the U.S. Navy), were finishing up the last details before setting sail for Milford, Connecticut. Rod primed the alcohol stove and lit two burners. He soon had a much bigger fire going than he expected—the whole stove and the shelf beneath it were engulfed in flames. Always cool and polite, Rod asked in an unruffled voice, "Will someone get me a bucket of water, please?" He quickly doused the fire. Mark up one advantage for alcohol.

By the time we had tightened up the loose flare fittings on the back of the stove and finished cleaning up and getting ready to go, it was 9:30 P.M. and cold.

When you sail with Rod, you go when the boat is ready—no matter what the conditions. *Loki* was ready, so we set the jib and jigger and sailed out of the harbor into Narragansett Bay, where we hoisted the main. Sally got us a late supper, and as she was taking the meat out of the icebox, she wondered if something was wrong, since the inside of the icebox didn't feel cold. Then someone pointed out that the cabin temperature was only forty-five degrees. No wonder.

Milford, Connecticut, was to be *Loki*'s home port. On the way there, we tried out all the sails made by Ed Raymond of Hathaway, Reiser and Raymond, and found that they fit very well. At one point, Sally let the spinnaker collapse for a few seconds. Rod's stern response was, "Sally, don't ever do that again!" She practically never has.

The next few weeks were spent sailing here and there to get the bugs out of various pieces of equipment, such as the stove and the stiff rudder.

There were also minor things to do, so quite often after a day on the job in the lab, I'd drive down to Larchmont to work on *Loki* for three or four hours, then come home and go back to work the next day. I wish I still had that much energy. Finally, we were off to Larchmont to try *Loki* out in the Storm Trysail Block Island Race.

The race was foggy with fluky northwest winds, and we made the mistake of rounding Block Island too close in, so that we were in the wind shadow of the cliffs on the southeast end of the island. We missed the tide in the Race on the way home and stayed more or less in one spot south of Fishers Island for five hours, but in spite of this, we ended up in third place after Paul Campbell's *Julie* and Harvey Conover's *Revonoc*. Both were highly successful veterans of cruising-racing, so we were well pleased.

After this encouraging start, Sally took *Loki* to New London, while I was at work, for the spring Off Soundings Race, with a couple of inexperienced friends for crew. They had a very slow upwind passage in thick fog, and on the way were so far up into Niantic Bay that they not only heard the New York–Boston train but actually got a glimpse of its lights through the fog. At this point, they thought it prudent to tack out again! They finally arrived at Burrs Landing in New London at three o'clock on Saturday morning, where the rest of the racing crew and I were waiting. Unfortunately, in spite of our disaster at Edgartown some years before, we had not read the race circular carefully enough, and it turned out that the race started Friday, not Saturday. We hastily put Sally's nonracing crew ashore and started through the fog at four o'clock for Shelter Island and the second day's race. Here we acquitted ourselves a little better, finishing sixth out of thirty-six. We hoped that no one had noticed our stupidity in missing the first day's race, but Commodore Blunt White took care of that when he was handing out the prizes. He began his speech with a long, hilarious, and detailed description of our race chasing, and left no one unaware of what had gone on. We were not happy to have this publicized, but Blunt never could pass up a good joke.

Jane and Walter Page were aboard as crew for the Vineyard Race that year. We first met Jane when she and a friend ran Foster Place, a small inn for young skiers at Stowe, Vermont. Both Walter and Jane had lots of racing experience, he on his father's NY 32 *Rampage*, and Jane on all sorts of boats. Her father, George Nichols, was skipper of the J-boat *Weetamoe*, which was narrowly beaten out for the defense of *America*'s Cup by *Enterprise* in 1930. Jane, as a teenager, had crewed aboard her father's Six-Meter *Goose* when she won the Scandinavian Gold Cup in Helsinki. We had a thoroughly experienced and expert crew.

When the time allowances were figured, we were fourth behind *Revonoc, Chanteyman,* and *Babe* out of seventeen starters. Not too disgraceful, but heartbreaking since we finished second, boat for boat in our class, and took almost an hour in a flat calm to sail the last mile of the course, only to have the breeze come up and bring the lower-rated *Babe* and Ed Raymond's *Chanteyman* roaring up to save their time on us. Even more heartbreaking was the later finding that our measurement certificate was in error, and that, if we had had a correct one, we would have won the whole race. Such is the luck of the game, and everyone can find an excuse for not winning.

In general, the bigger a boat is, the faster it sails. To make things fair in ocean racing, each boat is given a "time allowance" to be subtracted from its "elapsed time," to give a "corrected time" by which winners are determined and prizes are given. A series of complicated measurements of a boat are made (including length, beam, draft, sail area, rig, and so forth), and these are plugged into a formula or "rule" from which the "rating" and the time allowance are calculated. The Cruising Club Rule, created by the Cruising Club of America, was the one used for most overnight and ocean races in this country in the postwar years.

Loki's first year also involved some wonderful cruising, including our first offshore passage to a foreign land. We signed on Sterling Taylor, a graduate student in my department at Yale, and old friends Wister and Camilla Meigs of Woods Hole for a cruise to Nova Scotia. The first afternoon underway, Wister, Sally, and I spent a lot of time taking and working out sights, until they agreed with where we actually were. Sally and I had learned something of celestial navigation from her father, and we had also jointly (although the navy was unaware of her participation) taken a navy correspondence course in celestial navigation while I was on active duty in Maryland. This was our first chance to try out our new skill.

From Woods Hole, we sailed out around Cape Cod, passing Cross Rip Lightship, Handkerchief Lightship, and Pollock Rip Lightship on the way. They're all just buoys now, and a lot of the glamour they lent this passage has been lost. We saw lots of whales on the way, and one large one sounded about ten feet off the port bow and actually swam under *Loki*. There were also pods of porpoises and pilot whales or blackfish. By the second day, we were in the fog and followed our position down the coast with radio direction-finder bearings. Somehow these bearings, though useful, took some of the excitement out of the landfall, since they provided solid evidence that Nova Scotia had to be there before we could actually see it. They did, however, lead us to a position off Liverpool, and we sailed in as the fog scaled up along the land. We got a royal welcome, as only a few American yachts had come to Nova Scotia since the war. We were invited ashore for meals and baths, and the next morning were even presented with a bottle of milk by a young member of a local family.

Rod had suggested that we look up Angus Walters, the skipper of the famous Canadian schooner *Bluenose*, which had so decisively beaten the United States entry *Gertrude L. Thebaut* in the last International Fishermen's Races. When we got to Lunenburg, the chief fishing port of Nova Scotia and the home of *Bluenose* and Angus Walters, we went to see him and asked him to come for a sail with us the next day. He and his son accepted, and piloted us to Prince's Inlet, where there was a local race that day. Angus was all for taking *Loki* in it, but I pointed out that we weren't entered and hadn't been measured for the race. This didn't seem to matter to him in the least. He said, "We'll just follow the racers around the course." It turned out that we were too fast to follow, and were rapidly catching up with the other boats. At one point, I was sailing on the port tack with my view to starboard blocked by the genoa, while one of the legitimate racers was crossing us on the starboard tack with the right-of-way. Angus kept telling me I had plenty of room and not to bear off. When the racer finally appeared in front of me, our pulpit seemed to be over his cockpit, although I guess we missed him by four or five feet at water level. He and his crew looked really petrified, and I can't say I blamed them. This was not my idea of how to avoid interfering with the race, but Angus was totally unconcerned. All that day, he never mentioned anything about fishing, but only told us about the times he'd raced *Bluenose*. He'd sailed her over to England after the Fishermen's Race, and had been dismasted there while racing in a gale. When I said that we'd like to take *Loki* abroad some day, he assured me that she was much too small for such a venture.

Finally it came time to start home after a few lovely, sunny, and fogless days exploring the many islands of Mahone Bay. Our complement was down to three: Sterling, Sally, and me. After a foggy run to Liverpool, we set out direct for Mount Desert, using a watch system with six hours on and three off in order to have two people on watch all the time. After one clear day, we had the usual fog and southerly winds for the next couple of days to Mount Desert. The fog lifted as we approached the island, and we ran into Bar Harbor to officially enter the United States.

By this time, we were a little groggy and slaphappy from lack of sleep, and decided to go on that evening to Southwest Harbor, where we were to meet a medical school classmate of mine and his wife for the trip back westward. We ignored the very visible fogbank outside, since there was still a nice breeze at this point, but as night came on, so did the fog, and the wind dropped completely. After a long period of drifting, we decided to try towing *Loki* into Otter Cove, which I thought we could do at night in the fog by the sound of the breakers. I had run a rusty nail, which some thoughtful soul had driven through the pennant of the mooring at Bar Harbor, quite far into the palm of my hand, which had swollen up a lot, so I stayed aboard *Loki*, hoping that as we passed close to the mouth of the cove, which was bold on both sides, we would hear a decrease in the noise of the surf on the rocks. Unfortunately, this didn't work out, and after an hour of towing by Sterling and Sally, we gave up this idea. We drifted for a while and then wearily towed and sailed *Loki* up to a noisy bell buoy a couple of miles farther along, illegally tying up to it for the rest of the night, with Sally and Sterling alternating on anchor watch. I took advantage of my injury to sleep in, anesthetized with some scotch. The log says "lots of scotch."

The next morning, the fog was still with us and there was a

breath of air, so we cast off the buoy and started for Southwest Harbor. Once again, the wind fell, so Sterling got out the accordion to pass the time, and this had a profound effect on the lobstermen out hauling their pots. When they slowed their engines to pick up their pot buoys, they could hear the accordion, and they would come over our way to see what strange manner of boat sounded music rather than a foghorn. A series of boats loomed out of the fog, and then vanished, curiosity satisfied, back to their fishing.

We finally picked up Doro and Ethan Sims and had a pleasant evening with their family before starting westward the next day. To no one's surprise, the next day was calm and foggy. We drifted out the Western Way and over the Bass Harbor bar, where the fog scaled up a little, and on toward Swans Island with virtually no wind at all. The musical crew sang canons, rounds, and played the accordion, the clarinet, and the recorder until I, being quite unmusical, was ready for the madhouse. Then the breeze came in hard from the south, and with it more very thick fog. We got a quick bearing and estimated distance to the black spar buoy (now a gong) northeast of Swans Island, just before the fog obliterated everything. Swans Island and the anchorage at Atlantic was upwind from us, meaning that we would have to tack several times from a roughly estimated position to get into the harbor. We anchored so as to have time to work out proposed courses and distances to the harbor, then translated the latter into time and set sail again. After completing the planned maneuvers, we anchored once more, but could still see nothing but fog. I rowed the dinghy toward where I hoped to find the edge of the harbor, and, to my relief and delight, found we were just where we planned to be. It was still so thick that Sally had to keep blowing the horn so I could find my way back to *Loki*.

It was light and foggy again the next day, so we decided to abandon our plan of harbor-hopping and showing the Simses some more of Maine's beautiful coastline, heading homeward offshore instead. We sailed out through the lovely Orono Passage with fair visibility, but the fog soon returned and the breeze remained light. Two days later, we reached Gloucester in a sizzling heat wave, which so stiffened up our nylon mainsail that it never again was soft and easy to furl. The Simses had to leave us here, so Sally, Sterling, and I started on toward home.

Just west of the entrance to Gloucester Harbor, the breeze went permanently flat again, so we towed and drifted into Magnolia Cove behind Kettle Island, a mile or so farther along. This was a fairly exposed anchorage, but since the wind was nonexistent, it didn't really seem to matter. If the wind did come up onshore, we could always move, and we would have the motive power to do it. A canoe approached us with a man and his young son, so we asked them aboard. We gave them drinks while we cooked and ate supper. They seemed starved for company, and the father never stopped talking except to drink his whiskey. Eventually, we persuaded him we were too tired to come ashore and drink at his house, so he finally left. After a quick swim, we got thankfully into bed, only to be awakened around midnight by the same man bumping into *Loki*'s topsides with his canoe. This time he had a victrola with him and was playing old Al Jolson records. We took turns trying to get him to leave, but he'd improved each shining hour since his last trip to *Loki* with the bottle, so by now he was almost impervious to suggestions that he should go home and let us sleep. Even direct requests seemed to go over his head. Finally, we got him to go somehow, and went to bed again for what little was left of the night.

We continued our racing the next year with another third in class in the Storm Trysail Block Island Race and extended our range to the Newport-to-Annapolis Race, where we didn't do so well. The most fun on this venture was the trip home. We thought we were really in with the big-time racers as we sailed up Chesapeake Bay after the race, with George Clowes on *Golden Hind,* Bob Hall's *Nimrod* (his crew was delivered to Annapolis by Grumman Widgeon seaplane, which impressed us mightily), and Harry Morgan's *Djinn*. Later, in Cape May Harbor, we met *Infanta,*

Carina, Teal, Spookie, and *Burma,* all of whom were well-known ocean racers.

The upper bay was lovely, with enormous green fields coming right down to the water's edge, and the Chesapeake and Delaware Canal itself was much more like a river in those days, as it had not yet been widened by the Corps of Engineers. Our first sight of it was a steamer coming toward us, apparently out of the trees, as it rounded a bend into the upper bay. We picked up our ever-faithful crew member Sterling Taylor at Chesapeake City and spent the night in the anchorage pond dug out of the land on the outside of a bend there. It was fun to watch the steamers headed directly toward us about one hundred yards away, knowing that a piece of solid land separated us from them.

George Clowes towed us through the C&D Canal in *Golden Hind* and had planned to give us a pull through the Cape May Canal as well. Unfortunately, his engine gave out after we had both sailed down the Delaware River, and we passed him in the Cape May Canal.

We had a fair wind but a head tide in the canal, so progress was slow. It got a good deal slower when we came to the first highway bridge. The bridge tender had seen us coming and had opened the bridge a good half hour before we got there, although we hadn't yet blown for it. By the time we got between the bridge abutments, the automobile traffic was backed up for what seemed like miles on either side. Things soon became even worse, as the bridge blocked the wind and speeded up the current until we were standing still between the abutments. By this time, the bridge tender was frantic, and called to a Coast Guard surfboat, which was approaching with the current, to pull us out of his bridge. The surfboat tried to turn in front of us but misjudged the speed of the current, found he couldn't make it, straightened out, gunned his engine, and almost crushed us against the bridge pier. We had to fend off the pier on one side and the Coast Guard on the other. Needless to say, he didn't come back to offer us a tow again, and we pulled ourselves through with a boathook. The bridge tender was in such a state that he almost shut the bridge on our mizzen-mast. The next bridge was for trains and was already open. Luckily, it had a long ramp beside the pier, and we landed Sterling on it to pull us through with a line. No bridge tender, no help, no flap. We sailed on into the tiny inner harbor of Cape May, which seemed almost like sailing up a village street. It was surrounded by tiny shingled fish-houses on both sides.

On the way up the New Jersey coast, we sailed very close to the beach with an offshore breeze in lovely, smooth going. The forecast was for continuing westerlies, but about twenty miles south of Sandy Hook a very sudden shift to a hard northeast breeze came in and caught the genoa aback. We could only just lay the course now on starboard tack, and were in water so shallow that seas were almost breaking, making for an uneasy and wet sail hard on the wind that night all the way to Sandy Hook.

We stopped at Sheepshead Bay to ask about a tow through the East River, and found that it would cost fifty dollars, so we decided to sail through on our own. Sally had been dying to do this anyway. To begin with, we had a fresh southeast breeze. The New York skyline was very impressive indeed, but it also made the wind really fluky. Much to our surprise, the towboats seemed friendly and none of them crowded us. One even responded to our two blasts by honoring our intention to alter course to port. As we sailed up the river, the wind became unpredictable, and there was an ominous-looking thundersquall over Manhattan. The East River didn't seem to be an ideal place to be caught in a severe thunder-storm without power. I considered tying up at one of the docks on the Brooklyn side to wait it out, but they were so forbidding, with tarry pilings and rusty bolts sticking out, that we decided against it and took our chance with the thunderstorm. Fortunately, it never reached us, and soon we were reaching easily up the river again.

We sailed up the east side of Welfare Island and near the north end met a towboat skipper going south and obviously feeling no pain. He blew his whistle several times, put his helm hard over so that the towboat rolled almost rail down, and then came out of the pilothouse grinning, cheering, and waving wildly. He then repeated the whole maneuver in the other direction. He didn't come too close, and we couldn't help enjoying the tremendous fun he was having. After that we sailed on up the river, through Hell Gate, and into the Sound, to our mooring in Norwalk. Not long after that, we laid *Loki* up—more than satisfied with our new boat and the exciting life she provided for us.

4

The following year, 1950, we got into what was then big-time racing. Ed Raymond, who had made *Loki*'s sails, signed on for the Bermuda Race. He owned then, and still does, the fabulous *Chanteyman,* which, according to the song about her, "makes fools of the men who make rules, and likewise the race committee." In any case, Ed has won many more than his share of races in *Chanteyman.* He is sort of a "seat of the pants" genius in a boat. He doesn't always seem to pay too much attention to exactly where he is, and sometimes doesn't bother with cross bearings or very careful plotting of his course, but he has an inborn computer that keeps track of everything, and even if this isn't working, his luck takes care of the situation.

On one Off Soundings race, Sally and I were sailing with Ed from New London to Shelter Island. He was steering out of the Race in the fog, and we hadn't plotted a course yet, so he suggested I get out the chart and have a look. *Chanteyman* didn't have a chart table, so I used the cabin sole. There weren't any parallel rules, either, and Ed told me to use the "quick stick," which turned out to be a dowel with a couple of rubber ends on it like the fittings on the end of a cane. After rolling this around on the chart for a while and doing some figuring of time, course, and estimated distance, I guessed the next mark was about thirty degrees off the starboard bow. Ed said okay, changed course, and we found the mark. What was impressive was that the rest of the fleet, mostly bigger boats ahead of us, didn't notice our course change and went on sailing Ed's original course, knowing that he usually wins. We did win, by decoying them in the wrong direction!

Rod Stephens is just the opposite, as we found out racing on *Mustang.* He knows exactly where he is all the time. Everything is done with the utmost precision and forethought. If a squall looks as if it might reach *Mustang*, Rod takes a series of cross bearings, or, if these aren't available, gets an RDF (radio direction-finder) fix. Course, tidal set, and leeway are all carefully figured in. Rod even replaces his spinnaker halyard with a messenger (a piece of light line) when the halyard isn't in use, to reduce windage. Rod and Ed are at opposite poles in some of their approaches to racing, but both win with great regularity, probably because they both pay a great deal of attention to tactics and keeping the boat at maximum possible speed all the time. It was a great education for us to race with these two quite different but outstanding racers.

We had a super crew for the Block Island Race that year: Ed Raymond; Bill Dodge of Mystic—an old-time dinghy sailor and one of Harvey Conover's frequent crew members; Bob DeCoppet, owner of *Suluan;* and John White, owner of *Babe*. They all had great reputations in the racing world.

The race itself was one piece of good luck after another for us. The first night, the wind was very light, and we found ourselves among many of the bigger boats the next morning. As the breeze came in, they sailed away from us, but were held up at the Race by a head tide until we got there, when it turned fair for all of us. The wind went light again, and we had fog going around Block Island (which was always a plus for us since we'd done so much sailing in it) and we tried to keep the boat at maximum speed, while some others preferred to play it safer. After coming back through Plum Gut, Ed showed us how to get out of the head tide by playing the eddies very close to shore on the south side of the Sound. (I was so impressed with this maneuver that in the Block Island Race the following year, I got even closer to shore and managed to sail up one side of a very big boulder and down the other. *Loki* went right on sailing. Ed was with me in the cockpit having his breakfast orange juice and never spilled a drop. His only comment was, "Well, you know where it is now.") We ended up first in Class C, with many of the Class A boats and even more of the Class B boats not yet in, and were second in fleet to *Bolero* on corrected time.

Before going to Newport for the start of the Bermuda Race, we went to a dance on Long Island with Jane and Walter Page. At one point, I was talking to Lee Loomis. He asked me who my crew was for the race. When I told him that it included Sally, he roared with laughter and explained that girls didn't go in Bermuda Races. Some years later, when he had a Class A boat, and Sally had been in the crew of a Class C and a Class B winner, I took perverse pleasure in suggesting to Lee that he might like to have Sally in his crew to cinch a win in Class A.

I looked forward to my first Bermuda Race with great excitement and a very healthy respect for that passage. I'd been on a cruising trip to Bermuda with Sally's father on *Freya* in 1946, after I'd gotten out of the navy and Sally's brother Fred had gotten out of the army. Two other young men in their early twenties came along, but none of us except the skipper had had much offshore experience.

It turned out to be an eventful cruise. The bobstay turnbuckle backed off one night, leaving the bowsprit and head stay unsupported. The barrel of the turnbuckle was lost overboard, so we had to jury rig a tackle to hold the bowsprit down and stiffen up the head stay. The next night, when I came off watch, there was a strong smell of gasoline in the cabin at nose level. The coal stove, at waist level, was going full blast. When we tried to put it out with the carbon-dioxide extinguisher, it was so hot that it relit itself, so we filled the bilge with carbon dioxide to keep the gas fumes from exploding. Then we pumped and sponged the gas out, after turning off the supply, so no more could leak into the bilge through the sticking float valve in the carburetor.

As we approached the Gulf Stream, we could see that the northern edge was marked by a row of tall and narrow thundersqualls, so close together that they looked like the fingers of a giant hand. While furling the main for one of these vicious squalls, the topping-lift fitting aloft broke, and Sally's father, who had been leaning over the boom, came down with it and hit his head on the cabin house. This produced a nasty gash over one eye, and, like other head wounds, it bled copiously. When I asked Fred to hold a light so I could fix his father, he turned green and had to go quickly on deck. It was much too rough to sew up the cut, so I made do with adhesive tape. Then I found the skipper's blood pressure was up a bit, and he was also nauseated. Both these symptoms can be signs of a serious head injury, so, as ship's doctor, I kept him in his bunk. At this point we decided (wisely, I think) to turn around and head for home. With the skipper confined to his bunk, we were shy one watch officer, so I had to stay on deck for the next couple of days. Fortunately, we found out later that the skipper's elevated blood pressure and nausea were not the result of his head injury, and the cut was later hidden by his eyebrow, so I got an undeserved reputation as a plastic surgeon. After that experience, I couldn't help but wonder what the passage on *Loki* would be like.

We had the same crew for the Bermuda Race that we'd had for the Block Island event, with Bob DeCoppet acting as navigator. I was skipper as before, but I took Ed Raymond's advice on lots of decisions. Bill Dodge was also a very experienced racer, and I listened to his advice with care; and John White was an outstanding helmsman and sail trimmer. In fact, Sally and I felt a little bit as if we were on trial, since our crew had so much more racing experience than we had.

Because of, or perhaps in spite of, varying advice from all hands, we got a good start and were first over the line with our wind clear. There was a very fresh breeze, which gradually decreased, and as we got out toward Block Island, we shifted to the big genoa. *Loki* seemed a bit undercanvassed at that point, with the leftover bobble and a dying wind. The bigger boats gradually pulled ahead of us, and after that evening we saw no competitors and couldn't tell how we were doing in the fleet.

It turned out to be a relatively placid passage, not at all what I'd expected after the horror tales I'd heard of vicious thunderstorms and lightning in the Gulf Stream, and my own experience on *Freya*. My most vivid memory is tacking up to the finish line at night in a dying breeze. *Loki* seemed agonizingly slow, and I wanted to win so much that it was almost unbearable. I knew I was much too jumpy to steer in these conditions, so Ed sailed her, keeping his cool despite advice from all of us on how to make her go. From what the committee boat told us, it appeared that we'd won our class, on corrected time, with hours to spare from John Alden's higher-rated and bigger schooner *Abenaki,* and that we were the second boat to finish after her. It was only later that we found they had given us Greenwich time for *Abenaki*'s finish rather than local, and, in fact, we had only beaten her by three minutes and fifty-seven seconds—not much of a margin after more than six hundred miles!

We finished just after midnight on Thursday, four and a half days out of Newport, and started on our way to Hamilton. The first mark, according to the chart, should have been a flashing red buoy at the beginning of the channel. We found two fixed reds instead and decided it made more sense to anchor for the night outside the entrance to St. George's, rather than trying to find our way to Hamilton in the dark when the buoys and the chart didn't agree. Besides, it was time for a celebration, and this we felt was better carried out at anchor.

We were all delighted with how well *Loki* had behaved. The only disasters on the way were one episode of books falling out of the bookcase, a couple of annoying deck leaks over the starboard bunk, and three track slides chafed off the main. Hardly the horrendous life-and-death struggle that I had been half expecting before the start.

The next morning, Burt Darrel, who ran a boatyard in St. George's, came by in a big, gray ex-navy launch and offered us a tow through St. George's Harbor to Hamilton. We were delighted to accept, and Burt towed us through the passage edged with a shoreline of green trees and pink-and-white houses into St. George's harbor. We then picked up *Spookie,* another competitor built by Albert Lemos. She had engine trouble, so Burt towed us both through the very narrow channel into the open water of Great Bay and on into Hamilton. What a fantastically beautiful trip this was, with the color of the water running from deep blue outside, to brown, to a very light cream color in shallow water, depending on the depth and bottom. Burt brought us right into Hamilton harbor,

Loki *on the wind* (PHOTO BY BEKEN OF COWES)

all the more beautiful after our four and a half days at sea. On the way, Sally and Bob washed and polished the cabin so *Loki* would look her best for visitors in Hamilton. We anchored near *Mustang,* and Olin and Rod came by to reassure us that we really had won our class and offered their congratulations. We finally knew for sure that none of the smaller boats had saved their time on us. Then came a fistful of congratulatory telegrams and a lot of partying ashore.

Sally and I stayed ashore that night, and we'd just gotten back on board the next morning when Rod came by to warn us that the governor of Bermuda and his party were on their way to visit *Loki.* We got the rest of the crew out of the sack and organized, then shoved everything visible into any available locker to get her looking spick-and-span just seconds before the governor, his lady, and his aide arrived. We made appropriate polite noises, and they departed. Now we could all relax and enjoy our hangovers.

Eventually, we pulled ourselves together and sailed *Loki* across the harbor and into the dock to get water. During this maneuver, as one of the class winners, we were being photographed by the local newspaper. To make it look dramatic, we trimmed her in flat and bore off hard with the wind ahead of the beam. The photograph looks great until you notice from the pennant where the wind is coming from!

That night a prize-giving party was held, and Rod, as commodore of the Cruising Club of America, presented us with a silver bowl, the Thomas Fleming Day Trophy. There was a great deal of conviviality and filling of our prize with champagne supplied by the crew, and when that ran out, with anything that came to hand. This was shared by the crew of John Nicholas Brown's *Bolero,* second in Class A, and various other boats. Sally and I finally left, but apparently the party went on all night on *Loki* and *Mustang,* which was second in Class B to Irving Pratt's *Merry Maiden.* When we came on board the next morning, the crew was just cleaning up the cabin. Ed Raymond had had only twenty minutes of sleep, but was as cheerful as ever. That afternoon, Ed, Bill Dodge, Sally, and I set sail for home.

Winning our class in the Block Island and Bermuda races was certainly the high point of our sailing career so far. But it also left us with a slightly uneasy feeling that the glory wasn't so much ours, but really belonged even more to our crew and to the designers Olin and Rod Stephens. In those days, if you had a fairly new Sparkman & Stephens boat and didn't win, it seemed pretty obvious that you'd either had bad luck or hadn't sailed the boat as well as you might have.

Of course luck always plays a part in any race. For example, we now know much more about the big, circular eddies of current that exist on either edge of the Gulf Stream. If you get in one going the right way, great—but if it's a head current, it's not so good. Nowadays the varying positions of these eddies are known, but in 1950 it was guesswork. We had figured a Gulf Stream set to the east of about fifty miles, and tried to allow for this by going into the stream well to the west of the rhumb line. Beyond this, there wasn't a great deal of room for tactics, except to sail whichever tack was nearest to Bermuda as fast as possible. For this reason, I think the Bermuda Race is less interesting than coastwise races, where one can use tidal currents to advantage, trying to get into the back eddies and playing the onshore or offshore breezes as they change from daytime to nighttime.

In 1950, the ocean-racing group was relatively small. We all knew each other and were old friends. This was before the days of "factory teams" supplied to crew boats, making it very hard for nonprofessionals to win. It was also before the days when some of the crews were composed of "deck apes," who are sometimes hard to control at parties after the racing is over. Owners skippered their boats almost universally, instead of going along as passengers, as some do nowadays. All in all, it was a lower-keyed sport, much more amateur but still highly competitive, and, in my opinion at least, more fun than the modern high-pressure situation.

The character of racing-cruising boats has also changed a great deal since 1950, when a boat could stay competitive for a number of years. Today's "disposable" ocean racers, which cost enormous amounts, are competitive for only a season or two and then aren't much use for anything else, as they are too stripped-out below to be comfortable and their rigs are too flimsy to make good, safe cruising boats. As the popularity of racing has increased, much of the boat-buying public has set great store in owning boats just like the ones the hotshots are winning races with, even though they aren't going to race in top competition themselves. This leaves them with boats that are quite unsuited to their jobs.

Another thing that seems to sell boats is a large number of bunks. It's a puzzle to me why anyone who didn't have to would choose to cruise with six people on a boat less than 30 feet long. The vast expanses of cushions that look so appealing in manufacturers' brochures are much less so when they are covered with wet gear and crew members crawling around each other on their way to the head. When Hank duPont built his 45-foot *Cyane,* he put only five bunks in her because he wanted to prevent any possibility of cruising with two additional couples on board.

Nowadays, if you want to buy a stock boat for cruising, you are pretty well limited to either a spartan IOR type, or a clunker of the kind advertised as being able to "go anywhere." (Maybe they can, given unlimited fuel and time!) In my biased opinion, it's a shame the public doesn't have a chance to buy fast, able, wholesome, and comfortable cruising boats with modern underbodies, but without the lightness and extreme shape and rig that proved so tragically fatal in the 1979 Fastnet gale.

In 1949 I'd made the grade of being accepted in the Cruising Club of America. The CCA ran the biennial Bermuda Race and wrote the measurement rule used in many of the major races. This rule favored seaworthy boats, ideal for cruising or offshore passage making, as well as providing fair ratings for racing. It was a club for people who had demonstrated their ability to handle or navigate a small yacht offshore. To be accepted by this group was regarded by many, including me, as a real honor, since the cruising and racing heroes of that day were all members.

Norwalk, where we kept *Loki,* had a high concentration of Cruising Club members and a number of wags as well, so it was also the home of the Cruising, Boozing, and Snoozing Union. The CCA's burgee has a wavy blue line, representing the Gulf Stream, down the center of a white field. The Cruising, Boozing, and Snoozing Union had a wavy red line representing a corkscrew. The CCA awarded the coveted Blue Water Medal for outstandingly superior seamanship. The C.B. and S. Union awarded the Yellow Water Medal (a model of a lighthouse "to be lit when its owner was lit") for an outstandingly bad piece of seamanship. The CCA ran the Bermuda Race; the C.B. and S. Union ran the Singlehanded Creepstakes. To actually join this latter organization, one had, of course, to be proposed. In addition, the applicant had to give a long speech describing some past feat of horrendously bad seamanship to his peers in the assembled multitude. At my initiation, I was trying to get away with describing an episode that happened when I was commuting from New Haven to my job at New York University School of Medicine.

I bought a pair of roller skates in Grand Central Station in an effort to reduce the time spent in getting from there to the job. I sat down on my briefcase on the steps of a church on Forty-second Street to adjust the skates and put them on. Much to my disgust, a curious and unfriendly crowd collected to watch what seemed to me the interminable process of fitting the skates. I thought I'd lose them as soon as I got going, but, unfortunately, the first leg of the trip was uphill on Forty-second Street to Third Avenue, and all twenty of us progressed together in a group to the corner. The watchers maintained an interested but stony silence. From the corner, it was downhill to Forty-first Street, and I got away from the crowd, but soon realized that I really hadn't skated for a very long time and wasn't at all sure how to stop. Fortunately, there was a cop standing on the corner waiting for a green light, so I grabbed him and spun around him a time or two, losing speed. Just then the light changed. I thanked him politely and crossed the street, leaving him speechless behind.

Things seemed to go better for a while, until I picked up a drunk who was fascinated by the spectacle. I'd get away from him on the straightaway on each block, but he'd catch up as we'd stop for a light at the next crossing. We traveled together for several blocks this way until I got to an intersection with a green light and crossed ahead of him, only to fall flat on my back in the next block. A passing lady carefully walked around me, pretending not to notice me as I got up and dusted myself off before proceeding, still properly attired in my raincoat and carrying my briefcase, but also making some quite improper remarks about New York sidewalks. When I got to the lab, Colin McLeod, the department boss, was so intrigued that he insisted on trying out the skates, only to be met going around a corner by a technician going the other way carrying a tray full of glass petri dishes. Their crash was stupendous.

My story was met with laughter, but it obviously didn't qualify me for membership. It was stupid enough, but not nautical enough! I was just embarking on another made-up story, unlike the first one, which is true, of how I'd fallen overboard with an anchor in my hand on our honeymoon and only thought to let it go shortly before we both reached the bottom, when suddenly the lights went out in the living room where this was all going on, and the lawn outside was floodlit, revealing Sally in a flannel nightgown sitting on the seat of an outhouse and reading a Sears Roebuck catalogue, in full view of all of us. It turned out to be a well-staged joke with Sally's cooperation. Such was the C.B. and S. Union.

In 1951, the Creepstakes took place on a foggy day with an east wind. Forty-two boats were entered, each with one person on board. The biggest boat was a twelve-meter. As you can imagine, there was quite a jam at the starting line, and I was under the twelve. He had some wind, but I was effectively becalmed. I thought he'd get going fast and leave my wind clear, but it didn't work out that way. He sat on my wind for a long time before finally moving ahead.

The course went first to a can (no noisemaker) off Eaton's Neck, straight across the Sound and across the tide in the fog and traffic, with rocks and a beach beyond, then to the Cows buoy off Stamford, and finally back to the finish at Green's Ledge off Norwalk. Ed Raymond won, followed by John White in *Babe,* and then by

Rod in *Mustang*. *Loki* and I were sixth. The prizes included a pith helmet for the last to finish. It was decorated with a radio, earphones, weathervane, fake radar antenna, and whatever else the winner could find to decorate it with to improve his navigation before passing it on the next year. There was also a "Lucky Pierre Trophy" for "he who comes in in the middle of the fleet, showing that mediocrity pays."

After this start, the rest of the year was less exotic. *Loki* won her class again in the Block Island Race (despite her altercation with the boulder off Long Island). Sally's father was commodore of the Cruising Club, so we went on the club's cruise to Maine with the older two children. We were a bit concerned about having no power in Maine with the kids on board, in view of the high proportion of calms and fogs, so we took along an outboard motor, and mounted it on the Dyer dink, which we towed for the kids to sail. We used this with the bow of the dinghy pulled up close under *Loki*'s stern to push her along when needed. Once the engine was going, I could come back on board *Loki*, and the dink followed anywhere we steered. We kept our gas-and-oil mixture in Coke bottles capped by a machine bought from Sears. This fixed it so that there was no loose gas around and therefore no danger of explosion. We put gas in the engine, a bottle or two at a time, and ran it dry before getting it back on board. This was long before outboards with remote tanks and stern brackets were used on cruising boats.

One of the most memorable occasions of this cruise was sailing downwind in a stiff easterly through the very narrow entrance to Hadley Harbor, side by side with *Mustang*. The CCA fleet almost filled the anchorage. We both got our mains down in the entrance, made quick decisions about who to shoot up alongside, made our shoots and arrived successfully. My heart was in my mouth, and I hope Rod's was too, but I very much doubt it.

In Maine, we made many new friends and were introduced to a wonderful bunch of harbors, including Quahog Bay, McFarland's Cove, Naskeag, and Blue Hill. From Tenants Harbor to Camden, I sailed Holder Hudgin's *Infanta,* a lovely 50-foot Phil

Rhodes-designed boat, since Hudge had to go back to New York for business. When we asked around for a crew member to sail with Sally, there were several volunteers when they thought that they were going to be skipper of *Loki* (I can just see Sally allowing that), but they backed out when they found out they were only going as crew. She finally got a young cousin, Eleanor Folsom, to go long. *Infanta*'s engine refused to go for me, so we sailed her without it. It was fun to be in charge of a much bigger boat, especially with no power. Sally pointed out with delight in *Loki*'s log that she beat *Infanta* to Camden so badly that she had *Loki* anchored and furled up, with sail covers on, before I got there!

Our sailing season ended again with the Vineyard Race. When about five miles from the Vineyard Lightship, we met a good strong northeast squall that blew out the mainsail and the mizzen. We tacked up to the lightship under the storm trysail and jib while I sewed up the main on the boom to save time. I got soaked, but the job was done before we reached the lightship. We didn't want to blow it out again on the last of the upwind leg, so we hoisted it after rounding the lightship and roared home in fine style, ending up sixth in our class.

5

Nineteen fifty-two was a banner year for Sally. I had been asked to sail, at the suggestion of Ed Raymond, in the Block Island and Bermuda races on Phil Wick's *Mutiny II*. I asked Phil if he didn't want Sally too, but he said no, since his wife Greetie was going, and he felt one woman on board was enough. When Rod heard that we weren't taking *Loki* and that I was going on *Mutiny* without Sally, he immediately asked her to go on *Mustang* as one of his regular crew, not as cook. She jumped at the chance. In those days, Rod was the absolute "top of the heap" in sailing and racing. *Mustang* was certainly the boat to be asked to crew on. Some of the bigger boats might have had a better chance of winning the overall race, but Rod was the reigning expert. Wherever you went after a race, you'd hear people saying "Rod says this" or "Rod did that," and nobody wondered who Rod was. Sally was in seventh heaven.

Surprising as it seems now, Sally's mother was concerned about the propriety of her sailing without me on a boat with so many men. We reassured her that there was no time for hanky-panky on *Mustang* in an ocean race!

To no one's surprise, *Mustang* won Class B, but was second in fleet to Dick Nye's Class C *Carina*, much to Rod and Sally's anguish. We didn't do nearly so well on *Mutiny* in spite of Ed Raymond's presence, but we did sail into the harbor at Hamilton at night after the finish and were busy celebrating the next morning when *Mustang* came sailing in. For a brief moment we thought we might have beaten her, but it turned out that Rod had anchored for the night in St. George's harbor and come around to Hamilton in daylight. I decided to swim over to greet Sally and *Mustang* and managed, in my not-too-sober state, to fall off the bowsprit and take a good deal of skin off one leg on a whisker stay. When I

Mustang *(PHOTO BY MORRIS ROSENFELD)*

arrived wet and bloody on *Mustang*'s deck, I was greeted warmly by Sally, but with a little more reserve by Rod, who likes to keep *Mustang* spotless.

In spite of my bloody arrival, Rod asked me to sail back on *Mustang,* and since *Mutiny* had enough crew for the return trip,

I accepted with great pleasure. I found myself in the role of "the new boy at school" and kept asking Sally, *sotto voce,* how Rod liked this or that done. Rod, though he is a wonderful teacher, doesn't suffer fools gladly. There are different ways of doing things on different boats, so I was careful to learn to do things Rod's way on *Mustang*. There is nothing more annoying than someone who comes on board with a way of doing things that's different from the routine of that boat and goes ahead and does them in his own perfectly good but different way. The simplest thing, such as coiling a line and making it up in a nonstandard way, can be a real annoyance. If you want the line in a hurry in the dark and can't undo it because it's tied up differently than you expect, nerves get frayed and valuable time gets wasted.

Young Jimmy Dug, a nephew of Drake Sparkman, one of the founders of Sparkman & Stephens, was in the crew on the way home and lost a filling in one of his teeth. I had some equipment for such an emergency in my medical bag and was just about to begin operations when it occurred to me that human repairs were traditionally the skipper's job. I asked Rod if he would like to join in the fun, but his answer was to give me a disgusted look and disappear up on deck. So much for tradition. Jimmy ended up so pleased with my temporary filling that I had a hard time persuading him that he needed to get it properly done when he got home.

One weekend that fall, we were listening to Rod's tales of his early transatlantic crossings in *Dorade* and *Stormy Weather.* I wondered if *Loki* might be able enough to make such a voyage. At that time no yacht from the United States that we knew of had made a transatlantic voyage since the war. It seemed much more of an undertaking than it does today, when it's quite common and when there is even a transatlantic race every year or so. Rod said of course, *Loki* would be just fine for such a trip, and I belatedly realized that I'd talked us into a trap. If *Loki* was okay, then the only thing that would prevent us from going was our own inadequacy. This left only one possible decision—Go!

All the rest of that winter, Sally and I would occasionally get the "terrors," especially in the middle of the night. We'd wake up thinking, "Why in hell did we ever get ourselves into this jam?" We wondered how we would make out in a gale. What if we got dismasted? Would the food and water hold out? Suppose someone got really sick or badly injured—would I have enough equipment and know-how to cope? Since we had no engine, we couldn't carry a radio transmitter. We would be totally on our own and wouldn't be able to call for help, or have much chance of getting any from passing ships. We planned to stay north of the usual steamer lanes, both to avoid the chance of collision in the fog and because this was the shortest route to Norway.

Fortunately, we never had the "terrors" at the same time, and in fact rarely admitted to each other that we had them at all until much later. So the decision stuck, and we started the monumental job of making lists of everything we would need. We made lists and more lists and even lists of lists, all that winter, and these, incidentally, have been invaluable ever since for other long cruises and for lending to others who are planning long voyages.

For the food, Sally made up menus for a week at a time and then expanded them with variations to cover the four weeks we expected to take in crossing. She added an extra 50 percent for contingencies and emergency rations for a couple of weeks on top of that, in case of really bad trouble. We made lists of U.S. charts and ordered them for as far as Newfoundland and also for Great Britain. Rod lent us his old Norwegian charts from his trip there on *Stormy Weather* before the war. These were not available in the United States at the time, and U.S. copies were very crude, lacking the many-colored light sectors shown in true colors on the Norwegian originals. I checked over my medical bag and made it more complete. We took all sorts of spares, even including hot zinc terminals that could be put on wire at sea to repair a broken stay or shroud. This was before the days of the Norseman fittings, which we carry now. They are probably stronger and are certainly far easier to use. Fortunately, engine parts were not needed. I went to Coast Guard headquarters in New York to find out in detail about ice reports and the ocean-station weather vessels. Their radio signals indicated their positions on the grids—a hundred miles to a side—that they patroled. I asked about homing on such a vessel in the fog with a radio direction-finder, and the Coast Guard officer said, "Please don't do that, you might sink her." He was reassured when I explained *Loki* was only thirty-eight feet long and made of wood.

We also got a publication called *Nemedri,* which reported the presumed positions of unexploded mines in Europe left over from World War II. Being a wooden boat, we weren't going to explode magnetic mines, but there are contact mines too, and we certainly didn't want to blow up.

With no radio transmitter, the only way we could ease our families' worries during the voyage was to be reported by passing ships, if any, so we made arrangements with Lloyd's of London to clear the way for that. The routine was for us to signal a ship with code flags. She would then radio our position to Lloyd's, who would telegraph Sally's father's office in New York and charge us for it later. To be reported, we simply had to hoist the signal letters M I L in code flags, which means "please report me to Lloyd's," and then *Loki*'s name, also in code flags, when we saw a steamer.

All during the spring of '53, we polished and repolished lists and worked on *Loki.* We bought a rubber life raft, survival supplies, flares, and a Very pistol, and ordered a hand-sewn duck mainsail from Ratsey (the last one they made, I think). Stitches bury in duck, especially hand-sewn ones, and are less vulnerable to chafe than in synthetic sails, where the stitches stand up above the cloth. We also bought an expensive storage battery that had a very slow self-discharge rate to back up our regular one, which powered the electric running lights, the binnacle light, and a light in the head. Actually we didn't use the running lights on clear nights, except when we saw a ship, and that was rare. After crossing the Atlantic, we still had the slow-discharge battery in reserve and had only used up about half of the charge in our regular battery. Cabin lights were kerosene, except for a light over the chart table run by a six-volt "hotshot" battery and a similar one in the forecastle. Hotshots are the kind of batteries farmers use on electric fences. Over the sink, we installed a battery-operated fluorescent light fixture.

We expected it to be very cold where we were going, and it certainly was. Our cooking stove burned denatured alcohol, and did practically nothing to heat the cabin, so we bought a small Primus kerosene burner with a bronze bell over it. I rigged it up on the gimbaled table so it could be fixed in position when in use. It helped a little, but the cabin temperature was still very cold for the first half of the trip.

Everyone we dealt with during the preparations for the trip was wonderfully helpful. Nothing seemed to be too much trouble. Rod gave us much advice, lent us his charts, gave us the names of people to get in touch with, told us about currents in the Irish Sea for the Fastnet Race (our plan now included that), spent long hours going over our sail inventory and suggesting equipment to take, and told us about an excellent yard in Cowes. Bill Bedell, at his boatyard in Stratford, where we kept *Loki* that winter, also went out of his way to help in every way he could. This spirit of warmth and generosity was extremely touching and very much appreciated. Perhaps they all thought we'd never make it! In any case, it was obvious that people really cared and it made us proud and very pleased.

For crew, we got Bob Loomis, son of *Yachting* editor Alf Loomis, an old friend of Sally's mother and father. Alf gave us detailed and very helpful advice about strategy for the Fastnet Race, as he had sailed in a good many as navigator. Bob had sailed around the world with Irving Johnson on *Yankee,* part of the way as first mate. Someone suggested Dave Seeley, son of another Cruising Club member, who was just graduated from Yale. He came to the house, seemed to be a thoroughly nice guy with a good sense of humor, and had sailed across the Atlantic the year before on a French boat called *Janabelle,* so we signed him on too.

We remembered *Janabelle* from the Bermuda Race that year, mostly because one of her female crew had caused quite a sensation at the Coral Beach Club there after the race. She was a striking brunette, more than amply endowed, and swam in a white nylon bathing suit, which was the next best thing to transparent when wet. She drew quite a crowd when fresh out of the surf. I noticed that she kept going back in the water when she dried off, and when her admirers, many with cameras, began to thin out. When she emerged again, wet and visible in all her glory, the crowd always managed to return for one last look.

Davey told us that on the transatlantic crossing in *Janabelle,* the owner's wife gave a party halfway across for the crew, having promised them a big surprise. At the end of the meal, she came proudly out of the galley saying, "*Voila, la surprise, une crêpe enorme!*" The crew contained several Americans who couldn't help rolling with laughter at this remark. It desolated Madame to have her wonderful surprise greeted with laughter, and their explanation didn't particularly help either. A laugh on a long ocean race or passage is valuable in defusing fatigue and tension. Fortunately, things that wouldn't be worth a sick smile ashore can be hilariously funny at sea. It's even better if you can get a laugh from things that go wrong, so "Voila, une crêpe enorme" became a byword and greeted each minor disaster that summer.

One of the major problems for me that spring before *Loki*'s transatlantic cruise was that my mother had had a really uncharacteristic episode when she slept until eleven one morning. She usually woke up around six and only needed four or five hours of sleep a night. She seemed somewhat confused for a few hours after this, and then was much less active than usual. I got her to come to New Haven to see a doctor friend of mine, Gid DeForest, who could find no signs of what we both feared—a stroke—but she didn't seem to snap out of it and return to her usual energetic and vital self. I asked Gid if he didn't think I ought to give up the cruise to stay home with her, but he said no. He promised to take care of her, and told me that there were always lots of reasons why someone shouldn't do the really exciting things in life, but that most of them weren't valid. He went on to say that I'd always regret it if I let this keep me from going. I've always been deeply grateful to Gid for that piece of advice. That cruise in *Loki* was one of the really high points in our lives. Our opinion of ourselves in our subsequent lives would have been quite different if we hadn't made the trip. As it turned out, my mother was okay, and I wouldn't have accomplished anything by staying home. At one point, she seemed sort of blue about the trip, and I was explaining to her that there wasn't really any danger. "What's the point of going, then?" she asked, and I realized she knew perfectly well the appeal that a little risk added. Danger had never stopped her from doing extraordinary things. I knew she really approved of what we were about to do, even if it caused her some worry.

Another problem was that Sally had broken her arm in a touch-football game late in the fall. Our daughter Marianna told me that the snapping noise was so loud when it broke, that it scared the horse she was riding nearby. Sally had plenty of time to get this healed for the passage, but never did give it a chance. I remember her falling while skiing on a steep slope that winter and rolling down the hill with her arm still in plaster. She later rebroke it inside the cast while hanging up sheets to dry in the cellar when she grabbed for one that slipped off the line. The break was finally healed enough so that her orthopedist said she could come on the cruise if she kept her arm in a leather brace. She discarded it soon after the start.

The great day came at last, after most of the winter had been spent preparing for it. Even then we weren't completely ready. *Loki* was at the Norwalk Yacht Club, and both Bob Loomis's and Dave Seeley's families arrived to see us off before we showed up with the last two full station-wagonloads of food and gear. We tried to load it all on board while more family and friends arrived and brought more presents, which also had to be stowed somewhere. They included flowers for Sally, a bottle of Añejo rum from Alf Loomis, a world atlas (in case we got lost) from two members of my department in the medical school, a piece of rope to hang ourselves with if we shot an albatross (this from the same pair), and a whole turkey dinner from Dave Seeley's mother, plus whiskey, caviar and paté from my mother. In the midst of all this confusion, several newspaper reporters showed up. My mother, after a life in politics, had decided we weren't getting enough publicity, so she had told the papers about our proposed cruise. Sally and I both felt that the time for publicity was after the cruise was completed, not before it started. Imagine the embarrassment if we had to come back! I heard one of the reporters say, looking at a dozen gallon cans of alcohol for the stove waiting to be stowed, "They say they haven't got an engine, but what's all that gasoline for?" Finally, before they drove us crazy, Captain Black, the yacht club manager, hustled them into the launch and took them ashore.

After getting most of the supplies, clothes, and food at least down below, we hoisted sail with a fresh breeze from the northwest. As we dropped the mooring pennant at four o'clock on that afternoon of June 3, John Davis fired a saluting cannon from the deck of his schooner *Malabar III,* the assembled multitude cheered and waved, and we were off. John came alongside in *Malabar* and threw us some cold Heineken beer. What a send-off!

As we sailed east down the Sound, we went below by turns and began the seemingly impossible job of trying to stow all the gear, food, clothes, and supplies in some sort of reasonable order. We got pretty much everything put away except the charts, of which we had a total of sixty-six pounds, and then it was time for supper. Even though we were all tired, we decided to keep going rather than anchoring at Duck Island. The next morning, we just made it out of the Race with a fair tide, and as we left Long Island Sound, we met the small steamer *Inge* from Bergen, going in the opposite direction. This seemed like a fine omen for our cruise. When we passed the Vineyard Lightship close aboard, one of the Coast Guard seamen asked the routine question about the name of the vessel and her destination. We told him we were called *Loki* and were going to Bergen, Norway. He didn't answer, but ran down the deck to the door of the deckhouse, yanked it open, pulled another sailor out, and pointed to us, yelling, "Look, look, look, that boat's going to Bergen, Norway!" How different it is nowadays. On the way to the Azores in 1979, we were asked the same question by the Nantucket Lightship. We answered, "the Azores," and the reply from the lightship was a bored "Yeah, a fellow from Philadelphia bound for the Azores passed here two days ago. Have a nice trip."

We sailed into Woods Hole that night and spent a hectic next day on last-minute errands, sending extra charts home, arranging the remaining ones on board, stowing emergency water and food inside our dinghy and lashing it on the house, and finally sailing *Loki* into the dock for a final topping-up of her water tanks. We carried eighty gallons in two tanks, plus seven more in a big plastic demijohn called "the baby." After a full day of this, we went ashore for a farewell dinner and came back early for a last much-needed sleep at anchor before the long voyage. This was interrupted when Sally realized that she couldn't remember stowing the British charts, and thought perhaps we had put them in with the ones we sent ashore. Since it was easier to check those than the ones we had buried aboard *Loki,* she and I rowed in at six the next morning, before the rest of the crew was awake, and checked the return bundle. The charts weren't there, so we knew they had to be aboard.

We left Woods Hole under jib and jigger in a fresh southwest breeze with the "small boat" warning flag flying from Nobska Light as we passed. It made us feel very professional to ignore it and go merrily on our way. We had a lovely sail out by West Chop, Cape Pogue, and the string of lightships ending with Pollock Rip. All these marks, familiar from years of cruising, now took on a new and dramatic significance. As we left them one by one behind and set out on our great adventure, they were the last familiar things we would see for weeks to come.

We set up watches with Bob and Davey on one, with Bob in charge, and Sally and me on the other, using the so-called Swedish system of two 6-hour watches in the daytime and three 4-hour watches at night. Dividing up the day this way, you get at least one long sleep each 24 hours, and there is the further advantage that the watches are automatically dogged, which means that the duty hours are varied each day so that no one gets stuck with the same watches permanently. Sally was navigator, as well as standing watch with me, and started out at first doing all the cooking. We finally persuaded her to let the watch on deck cook and the new watch coming on after the meal do the cleaning up. This worked out much better. Sally is a real iron woman on a boat, and on one Bermuda Race, she did combine the jobs of cook, navigator, and watch officer successfully. But she needed *some* rest on this much longer trip, and luckily Davey and Bob turned out to be most ingenious at preparing really excellent meals out of the canned food that made up most of our supplies. With no refrigeration, the only fresh foods we could keep were things like potatoes, onions, apples, oranges, and eggs.

The first week was cold, wet, windy, foggy, and just a little discouraging. The fact that *Loki* was leaking a bit, and one keel bolt was loose and could be turned freely in its hole, making it impossible to tighten, didn't help. (Luckily the wood around it swelled up later, and the bolt tightened itself.) I think every one of us privately felt a little gloomy on the fourth and fifth days out, but no one mentioned it, and it was soon forgotten as we settled into the routine of offshore sailing and learned to live with the cold.

The cold and fog were the result of the Labrador current running southwest between the land and the Gulf Stream, which flows in the opposite direction. Labrador current water is cold and has icebergs in its northern part in early summer. Bergs have even been seen as far south as Bermuda in really bad ice years. The Gulf Stream, of course, is warm, with water temperatures reaching eighty degrees and more off our Eastern Seaboard. When the air, warmed and saturated with moisture during its time over the Gulf Stream, is blown over the cold water of the Labrador current, it gets chilled and has to give up some of its water, which precipitates out as fog. This is the reason fog is so prevalent with southerly winds along the northeastern part of our continent and Newfoundland in summer.

The Great Circle course to Bergen from Woods Hole crosses the land well north of Cape Sable (southeast end of Nova Scotia) and of Cape Race (southeast end of Newfoundland). We put down an arbitrary "Point Able" on the chart, indicating the southern boundary where ice might be expected, and drew our course to it from the Pollock Rip Channel. This also kept us safely clear of Cape Sable and Cape Race. From this point we drew our Great Circle to Bergen. A Great Circle course is the shortest distance between two points on the earth, and is perhaps easiest to understand by stretching a string between the two points on a globe. The string traces a Great Circle course. If you do this between Cape Cod and Bergen, you'll notice that the string cuts the longitude lines at very different angles near the beginning and end of the imaginary voyage, starting at approximately northeast, and ending a little south of east. A Great Circle course, in all but special cases, has constantly changing compass directions as it progresses, but in actual practice the course is only changed periodically, depending on the speed of the vessel. Great Circles can be figured out mathematically, or can simply be plotted on special Great Circle charts. When we plotted our course to Point Able, we found it went right through Sable Island, off the east coast of Nova Scotia, and we chose to go west of this low, sandy island, which is surrounded by wrecks of ships that have gone aground there.

At night, halfway between Sable Island and Nova Scotia, we were in the midst of thunderstorms. I happened to be alone on deck when *Loki* was hit by lightning. After the crash and flash, which occurred together, I was momentarily blinded and deafened. No harm was done, as *Loki*'s shrouds were well grounded with copper tubing to the keel bolts, so that she could be hit without serious damage, and I soon recovered. I was more concerned about *Loki*'s condition than my own for a very good reason. If I'd been permanently deafened or even blinded, it wouldn't have been the end of my life, but if *Loki* had sunk, it might well have been the end for all of us. The welfare of your boat offshore has to come first. Without her the whole crew has a very tenuous future at best. Even so, it is not an experience I particularly want to repeat. I'm beginning to wonder if I have a magnetic personality, since I've also been in an airplane and a house that were hit by lightning.

On the sixth day out from Woods Hole, our receiving radio,

which also served as a direction-finder, quit cold. This meant no more ice reports and no more time-ticks to check our single chronometer watch by. Accurate time, of course, is essential for determination of longitude, and we could not rely on our chronometer without the radio, since its rate had been irregular. With a single chronometer, especially one whose rate was changing, it was extremely important to have time-ticks from station WWV, then in Washington. So we decided to go into St. John's in Newfoundland to have the radio repaired.

That night the fog came in again from the north, looming like a high, gray arching wall, absolutely solid, dead ahead of us. It was one of the most ominous-looking things I had ever seen from a boat. The only problems it brought, though, were near-zero visibility and frigid temperatures. It was very close to freezing, and, as an added bonus, it wasn't clear from the ice reports we'd gotten before the radio quit whether or not the ice was between us and St. John's. We found out later that the ice had actually been on the other side of Newfoundland, but we didn't know it then, thanks to poor radio reception and the very thick Irish brogue of the man who was doing the reporting. I stayed on deck all that night worrying about ice, and we took turns standing on the bow with our gloved fingers stiffening around the head stay, keeping a lookout ahead in the hope that we might see an iceberg before we hit it. It was a long, cold night. The fog cleared late the next afternoon, revealing the steep headlands on the shore and the entrance of a little fjord containing Fermeuse Harbor. We were all tired and looking forward to a night at anchor, and it looked too tempting to pass by. We sailed into the beautifully protected harbor, surrounded by high hills that flowed steeply into it. There were patches of potatoes growing on the hillsides, with their furrows running up and down instead of across. It looked to us like an invitation to erosion, but at that point we weren't about to start criticizing local agronomy.

We anchored near a small fishing schooner and were soon visited by some Fermeuse inhabitants in two enormous dories almost as long as *Loki*. We invited the men aboard. They were dressed in dark suits, apparently for some dour Saturday-night occasion. They seemed interested in *Loki,* but were very reserved and unsmiling. We offered them a drink, which they downed in one quick snort, leaving us sipping ours and feeling a little inhospitable in the somewhat strange and somber atmosphere. The obvious thing to do was to pour them another, which we did, and that also disappeared immediately. This went on as long as the booze lasted and without the slightest visible change in the unsmiling mien of our visitors. Shortly after the last bottle was emptied, they departed, still apparently unaffected but leaving us reeling. We finally had dinner at nine-thirty that night with a second somber group looking on but not partaking.

The next day was glorious, sparkling, and sunny, with wind off the land. We had a superb smooth sail along the very dramatic coastline up to St. John's. Here, we sailed through a narrow passage between the headlands leading into a completely enclosed big harbor. We anchored for the night near a hospital ship belonging to the Portuguese fishing fleet, which in those days came over every spring to fish for cod out of dories on the Grand Banks.

After a night at anchor in St. John's, we got up the hook and sailed to the Job Fisheries Dock to get the radio repaired and stock up again on fresh food and water. Carl Vilas, a Cruising Club friend of Sally's father and of ours, had a sister in St. John's who was married to the head of the Job Fisheries, so we had the red-carpet treatment, including a bath at their house for Sally and a tour of St. John's and environs in a chauffeur-driven Rolls-Royce. The Job Fisheries seemed to own the town, and Mr. MacPherson, who ran it, put all his facilities at our disposal. The radio was quickly taken care of, as were all our other needs, so that we were ready to go by late that afternoon.

It had been a wet and drizzly day, and I spent most of it working on the boat. As I worked, a group of locals dressed in heavy woolen pants and sweaters, but without raincoats in spite of the drizzle, looked down from the dock at *Loki* and shook their heads, making cheery remarks like, "I wouldn't want to go offshore in that." Or simply, "They'll never make it." I wasn't particularly looking forward to going out late that afternoon myself, knowing that it would be cold and wet with the fog waiting just outside. The optimists on the dock didn't make the prospect of setting off that evening any more appealing either, but time was a-wasting and we had a schedule to keep, so set off we did. As expected, we were quickly swallowed up in the wet and the cold and the fog. On top of all this, we found an almost flat calm for the first couple of hours after we had sailed a mile or two from the harbor. It took a good deal of determination to resist the temptation to head back to the warmth and comfort of St. John's that night.

6

Our course to Norway from St. John's started over the Grand Banks. This is an area with depths less than a hundred fathoms that extends south and east of Newfoundland for about three hundred miles. The Banks are one of the world's most productive fishing areas and were probably fished by many different Europeans long before Columbus "discovered" America. Anyone who found such a fabulous fishing ground wouldn't be eager to advertise it, so these early voyages didn't go down in history, except for those of the Vikings, who established colonies in Newfoundland. In those days, the Banks were almost alive with cod, which could be caught on long trawls of baited hooks. Preserving them with salt made it possible to take them back to Europe, where meat was a delicacy for the rich, and salt cod, or bacalao, brought a very good price. This made the rigors and dangers of a trip to the Banks worthwhile.

The dangers were and still are real enough; gales aren't rare, and hurricanes occasionally cross the area. The shallow water makes for steep and breaking seas, and icebergs float down across the banks in early summer. To complicate matters further, the incidence of fog reaches 40 percent in June and is only a little less in the months before and after.

The last of the Europeans to come under sail to fish on the Banks were the Portuguese, and they were still doing it when we sailed out of St. John's. We saw their square-rigged hospital ship anchored in the harbor, but the rest of the fishing fleet, mostly schooners, had left before we came in. Alan Villiers had made a six-month voyage on one of the numerous three- and four-masted Portuguese salt bankers a few years before, which he described in *The Quest of the Schooner Argus*. The fishermen at that time still set their trawls from open dories launched from the mother ship.

On *Argus* they started at four in the morning, one man to a dory, and fished alone all day, only to come back to gut, split, and salt the catch, rebait their hooks at night, and then set off again at four the next morning. The trips lasted six months or more, so the fishermen never saw the summer in Portugal. The pay for the whole trip was only six or seven hundred dollars, even for the best fishermen, and the danger of being lost in the dories from rough seas or in the fog was always present. A very rough life for very tough men.

Compared to this, our trip was a picnic. Even so, the cold, the steep, short seas, the threat of unreported ice (small bergs are hard to spot from the airplane patrols), and the fog remained.

The calm we found just outside St. John's was soon replaced by an increasing breeze. By the next morning, we were tearing along in a strong fair wind, still enveloped in the cold and clammy fog, and planing down the steep seas with the optimistic speedometer going past eight knots on the first turn and up to four or five on the second time around the dial. Perching on the top of one of these seas was a little like the wonderful feeling of anticipation on the top of a very steep ski slope, and the schuss down was just as exhilarating.

This particular cruise with this particular crew was extraordinary in that all the way across the Atlantic there was a sense of great peace. There was absolutely no human conflict. We were totally absorbed with the same desire, which was to take care of *Loki* and get her across the ocean as well as we could. This made for a sense of unity, and we shared a feeling of total independence from the rest of the world and its problems. We alone were in charge of all the world we could see, as far as the horizon or the nearest bit of fog. We were our own bosses and our responsibilities were only to *Loki* and each other. We would either make it to Norway or not, depending on our own skills and abilities, and if the luck or weather were too impossible, we'd at least have done our very best. Beyond that it would be in the lap of the gods, but I think we all felt we'd do a pretty good job up to the point where they took over. The sense of fulfillment was so strong that as we approached Norway, we were reluctant to end the cruise and its companionship, knowing that when we got there, wonderful as Norway was going to be, we would lose our peace and independence when the problems of the shore inevitably arose.

Months later, when we were in Cowes, the closeness we had felt offshore was brought home to us when some new crew members arrived from America. *Loki*'s cabin was pretty small, and six of us were getting dressed to go ashore to a party. Sally had gotten into her dress in the forecastle, but was having trouble with the zipper in the back. She came into the main cabin and asked Bob, who was nearest, to zip her up. One of the new crew made a joking remark about this being pretty cozy, and Bob was really angry that anyone could pretend to misunderstand the nature of the companionship we original crew members shared.

Sailing in *Loki* on the banks was very cold, just as we had expected—cold sitting on deck steering or just sitting, and cold down below. One of our problems was that it took a half hour to get dressed to go on watch, and our time for sleep was shortened. Under our oilskins and boots we wore two pairs of woolen socks, one long set of cotton and one set of woolen underwear, generally two pairs of pants, at least one of which was wool, a flannel shirt, a sweater or two, and a short quilted jacket, as well as woolen and leather mittens. Even dressed like this, we were cold sitting, but when we had to handle sails, we moved slowly and clumsily, and soon broke into a heavy sweat. It took me almost half an hour one night to put a reef in the main—a job that might normally take ten minutes. Afterward, I was clammy and exhausted.

Down below it wasn't much better. The Primus stove helped to dry out socks and mittens hung over it on temporary clotheslines strung across the cabin, but really didn't do much to heat the cabin as a whole, which was not much above forty degrees for most of the first week. This isn't cold, of course, compared to the temperatures people ski in, but sitting still for long hours at this temperature in damp air with no sun to warm you is quite different from exercising hard in crisp, dry air. We all took tremendous pains not to get our clothes wet, since there was no way we could dry any appreciable quantity of wet sweaters or pants in a cabin as small as *Loki*'s at such low temperatures. At the speed we were sailing, there was constant spray coming over, and no one, on pain of death, was allowed to go on deck without foul-weather gear, nor did we walk around the cabin in our socks. The damp cabin sole would quickly have gotten them wet and insured cold feet and wet boots.

Five days out, the fog and the rain cleared and the sun came out, so we were able to get morning, noon, and afternoon sights. Sally wrote in the log, "Still cold, but a definitely bearable kind. Water temperatue 42–44 degrees F., air temperature 44 degrees F." We saw our first ship but did not get close enough to be reported.

The next day the barometer began to fall, and we shortened down to jib and jigger as the southerly breeze picked up. The barometer kept falling, and the breeze kept increasing, bringing bigger seas. We were getting more and more spray on deck until at one-thirty in the morning, when I was alone on deck, a big sea came aboard, shoving me aft to fetch up against the mizzenmast three feet aft of where I'd been sitting. It filled the cockpit and seemed to be running out very slowly through the scuppers, so we bailed it out with a rubber bucket we'd brought along for just this purpose and decided it was time to heave to. We set the trysail trimmed not quite flat, the storm jib trimmed to weather, and dropped the mizzen. Under this rig, *Loki* eased along on her course at two knots with no one steering. We all went below to catch up on our sleep, but took turns, one at a time, standing two-hour watches below, fully dressed in oilskins, and occasionally sticking our heads out on deck to make sure there were no approaching steamers. This made us feel better but probably didn't serve any other purpose, since the visibility was so limited that we couldn't have seen a steamer in time to do anything about it anyway. Those of us in the forecastle bunks got quite a ride in those rough seas. One minute we felt as if we weighed a ton as *Loki* surged up the front of a wave, and the next we floated weightlessly as she plunged off the top of it. In fact we could turn over in the air on the biggest seas. Apparently, if you are tired enough, you can get used to anything, because sleep we did.

The next morning Sally's comment in the log said: "Seas are beautiful, steep, confused, and bright green where they break over the portholes. It's a dramatic and lovely sight, even though tinged with wonder as to how much worse it will get." The barometer had already dropped half an inch in the twelve hours before we hove to, and it continued the drop to reach a full one-inch fall in the next twelve hours. None of us had ever seen such an extreme drop, except in a hurricane, so there was ample reason for Sally's wonder.

It's very hard for me to tell just how hard it's blowing. I hear people say with great assurance that it is blowing sixty miles an hour, but when I ask what sails they have on, it turns out to be the full main and genoa. We shorten down to working jib and mizzen, with no main, in what I guess is thirty knots in *Loki* or *Loon*. In this blow, however, we did have some confirmation that we had really been in a hard gale. The winter after our transatlantic cruise, I was talking to the captain of the Coast Guard's square-rigger *Eagle*. He told me about the bad gale he had been in with her the previous summer, and how worried he had been about his cadets. It soon became obvious that he was talking about the same blow we were in, and that we had been close by at the time. His concern on a big square-rigger indicated that we hadn't overestimated the strength of the gale, and that Sally was quite reasonable in wondering a bit when the seas were breaking green over the deck and the ports in the side of the house!

Fortunately, the breeze didn't increase much more, and by the following morning it had eased off enough so that when I came back on watch, I found that Sally had put the mizzen back on while we slept. (This was not something I was very happy about. I don't like anyone alone on deck to go out of the cockpit without both a lifeline and letting someone below know, especially at night and in a blow.) The mainsail and working jib soon followed. That night before supper, I declared a party, which meant that we each got a tot of Alf Loomis's excellent rum. We had saved that, at least, from the thirsty Newfoundlanders!

By this time we had gotten far enough north so that the sun hardly went below the horizon, giving us at least sunset light all night long. Perhaps it was the midnight sun, or the effect of the rum, or maybe we were still a little silly from the storm. Whatever the reason, there's a note in the log saying, "Overheard from the port watch (Dave Seeley): 'It's getting lighter in the northeast than in the northwest. The sun must be rising faster than it's setting.' "

In general, I don't believe in drinking under way. This was our first party at sea since leaving home, but after this, I must admit, we found increasingly frequent reasons for a celebration: one-third of the way across, a birthday, halfway across, and we even extended this by considering halfway from Norwalk and halfway from St. John's. We ended up finding a good excuse to have one every two or three days, and they were a great morale booster, something to look forward to in this very cold and hard going. But each celebration was limited to a single drink, a far cry from the old British Navy tradition of half a pint of rum per man per day.

As we got further east the wind and seas gradually diminished, and by the tenth day out we were able to come on deck without oilskins for the first time. The temperature was much warmer too, now reaching fifty degrees in the daytime. That night, Sally's comment in the log said, "Moon has risen full and yellow. Man in the moon looks happier tonight."

On the next watch Bob said in the log, "Moon shone, stars twinkled, midnight sun, sky shimmered, seabirds fluttered, school of blackfish came up around us and blew. An enchanted hour."

As the weather gradually improved, so did our menus. The log reads for one evening that "dinner was a party—cocktails, canapés, ripe olives, nuts, lobster and crabmeat Newburg, rice, peas and carrots, strawberry shortcake." Who wouldn't sell a farm and go to sea?

Now we began to get English, French, Norwegian, Dutch, and

German broadcasts on the radio. It seemed very odd that our little portable receiver had learned to speak all these foreign languages so quickly. As far as we were concerned, we were drifting in a fog that might have been anywhere, but it certainly didn't seem alien. There was no feeling at all of being in a foreign country or even near one, and yet all this strange mixture was coming out of the radio. We have found this one of the great delights of going to foreign lands in your own boat. You can have the adventure of being in new and strange (to you) places, and at the same time feel secure and at home in your own surroundings.

With the warmer weather, it was time for a saltwater bath. Off came the quilted jackets, the double pairs of socks and trousers, and many layers of shirts, sweaters, and underwear. The water was good and cold when scooped up in a drop bucket and poured over our heads, but the feeling of being clean and fresh was well worth it.

We'd been listening for the weather ship on the radio for several days and hoped to go close by her, both to be reported to Lloyd's and to get an accurate position to check our navigation. The night before our baths Sally picked up her signal underneath a much louder station on almost the same frequency. Once we recognized the pitch of the beacon, it was easy to hear, but it was so low that one of the crew said it sounded like someone squeezing toothpaste out of a tube. We knew the weather ship could be anywhere in a square a hundred miles on a side, and that she sent out a coded signal to indicate which ten-mile square in this big area she happened to be in. When we finally recognized the signal, it told us exactly where to look. Shortly after we finished our baths, she popped up on the horizon steaming slowly in our direction. We hadn't expected her quite so soon, because she had been broadcasting a position ten miles farther east until shortly before we found her. We hoisted our M I L pennants asking to be reported, but the water was so smooth and the wind so light that we were able to converse with her as we went by, asking her to report us, which she agreed to do. Most of her crew was lined up at the rail to look at this odd specimen of a small boat so far from shore.

They were all very friendly and asked us if they could do anything for us, to which we replied, "No, many thanks, nothing beyond reporting us to Lloyd's." I felt a little bit stagestruck with so many people staring at us and stupidly asked them if there was anything we could do for them. Maybe I was remembering the time Joshua Slocum, sailing in pirate-infested waters in *Spray,* met a United States battleship and signaled a suggestion that they "should proceed in company for mutual protection."

The breeze continued to die, and the sea was glassy, with a big leftover swell. We'd had fulmars following us all the way once we were well out of St. John's. They had been flying and gliding around us, but now we were going so slowly that they flew ahead of us, landed, watched us sail by, then took off and flew ahead of us over and over again. Finally, we were almost totally becalmed north of the Shetland Islands. Here we made our worst day's run, twelve miles in twenty-four hours, and the fulmars were now fifty or a hundred strong, swimming along quietly in our wake.

For July 1, Sally wrote in the log:

> Shark day. It started on midnight watch for us, with light enough at midnight for me to read aloud to Giff from *Arms and the Man.* Even this wasn't enough to keep him awake, so he snoozed in the cabin while I had a happy two-hour trick at the wheel, singing all the arias and lieder that I could remember, and watching the wildlife start its new day. Five big sharks were close at hand, and a small school of porpoises, a silly big white bird (maybe a gannet) who tried and tried to get flying speed off the water. I could hear him making periodic attempts for minutes after we drifted by. There were also groups of little puffins, which completely enchanted me. They look like compact little bathtub toys. Three skuas also showed up this morning. After breakfast, the other watch was slow getting to bed, and before they managed to do so, some

> of the big sharks came very close. They were mammoth monsters, 20 and 30 feet long and about 5 feet wide, with mouths gaping at least 3 feet across. They looked dark with greenish spots around their heads. Their big dorsal fins were about eighteen inches high.

These basking sharks eat plankton, which they filter out of the water as they swim close to the surface with their mouths wide open. I'd been explaining all this, including the fact that they were harmless and didn't have anything but tiny teeth, when Sally said, "Well, why don't you put the dinghy over and chase one for the movies?" This seemed reasonable, and Bob and I went after one. When we watched the movies later, it was clear that the closer I got to him, the slower I rowed. A shark twenty-five feet long looks enormous from an eight-foot dinghy. It doesn't matter whether he has any teeth or not. It soon turned out that there was some question about who was chasing who as the shark got his head right up under the stern of the dink and came along whichever way I went. Harmless or not, he was starting to make me nervous. I slapped an oar on the water and he disappeared. This irritated Bob in the stern of the dinghy who said he was just beginning to get some good pictures! When we got back to *Loki* there were three sharks following her, one with his nose right up under her counter. His head was just as wide as *Loki*'s stern.

The next remark in the log after the shark episode was "Mardon Me Padam but this pie is occupewed. May I sew you to another sheet?" This just goes to show what happens to your mind after two weeks at sea.

Eventually, the breeze began to pick up, and we pushed on toward our landfall in Norway, an island called Holmengraa, north of Bergen. As we approached the coast, the sky had been overcast, and we hadn't had any sights of the sun for a total of four days. We were, however, taking Consol bearings on Stavanger in Norway and Bushmills in Ireland. Consol is a radio bearing system used in Europe. It's received on the standard broadcast band and consists of a series of dots and dashes, which, depending on the number of each, give you a bearing from the station. We were concerned that the bearings didn't check with our dead-reckoning position. Finally, on the afternoon of July 2, the sun came out intermittently, and Sally took a series of sights that agreed almost exactly with her dead-reckoning (DR) position, plotted from her last sights taken four days before. We found out later that the Stavanger station had been moved, which explained a lot. Sally keeps a meticulous DR position, plotting each change of course and distance run, no matter how short, so it was no surprise that it was the Consol bearing that was wrong.

We reached in toward the coast with the big genoa set, and at 4:42 in the afternoon we sighted land—distant mountains off the port bow. The next three hours were good and tense as we tried to identify the coastline, with its dozens of islands. We were tempted to alter course several times but hung on. Suddenly, dead ahead of us was a square white lighthouse, just like the little picture on the British chart. Sally wrote, "That was an exciting moment for the navigator," and continued, "The coast looked more and more beautiful as we approached, with the clouds lifting away, letting the late afternoon sunlight burnish everything with its gold-bronze light."

At 8:13 that evening, we were abeam of Holmengraa. We had crossed the Atlantic and once more were sailing with the much more immediate dangers of hidden rocks and the chance of losing our way through the unfamiliar islands. In spite of this, the sail to Bergen was one of the most beautiful I've ever had. The sunset with its brilliant colors lasted all night, gradually shifting its bearing to become the sunrise. The moon rose, incredibly soft and pink, and hung low over us for the whole night. It never got too dark to see the shoreline and the rare channel markers.

The Norwegian charts Rod had loaned us, with the beautifully colored light sectors, didn't help us as much as expected (though they were far better than the U.S. ones), since the lights had been turned off in summer to save electricity. We knew that the German battleship *Scharnhorst* had been sunk somewhere in Norway during the war and wouldn't be shown on our borrowed prewar charts. I had visions of running aground on her! One does worry sometimes about the damnedest and most unlikely things, especially at night. We didn't worry about changes in the aids to navigation, though, because the Norwegian ones are pretty permanent, consisting of lighthouses, called *fyrs,* smaller lights (*lygts*) on shore, and stone pillars on rocks or small islands called *vaarde.* The latter frequently had an arrows pointing to the channels. Buoys were rare. I don't think we saw half a dozen the whole time we were in Norway.

The breeze held until about two miles from Bergen. We rounded Hgellskjaer at the entrance to the harbor at one-fifteen that night, then tacked slowly up the harbor in the dying breeze. It was three-thirty before we reached Bergen itself. It looked unbelievably lovely, with its bold rocks coming down to the water and green fields with lots of trees. How beautiful green is when you've been at sea for a long time!

Harvey Conover, owner of the famous *Revonoc,* who was to sail with us in the Fastnet Race later that summer, had asked me when we were going to get to Bergen. I picked a time out of the hat and said two o'clock in the morning on July 3. By pure dumb luck, after three thousand miles, we were only an hour and a half late.

We sailed around the big harbor and finally found the yacht anchorage mentioned in the British Norway Pilot, picked up a mooring, put *Loki* neatly away, and, thanks to twenty-four hours without sleep, celebrated in a maudlin fashion in the bright morning sunshine before going to bed about 6:00 A.M.

It was a very short sleep. Customs came on board and woke us up at nine-thirty. They were very pleasant, quickly got us all straightened out, then asked the classic question that we heard all over Norway: "How are things in Brooklyn?" Apparently most Norwegians have either been there or have relatives there. After they left us, we went back to sleep for another hour, and then some reporters came out. It was four o'clock that afternoon before we finally rowed ashore after putting *Loki* in apple-pie order. As we climbed the winding staircase in the yacht club, I, for one, could still feel the roll of the sea beneath my feet and had to hold on to the handrail to keep my balance.

We were apparently the first American yacht to sail transatlantic to Norway since the war. The Norwegians were still grateful to the Americans for helping them beat the Germans, and they gave us a really warm welcome. We found out later that Norway had been expecting the U.S. ambassador to arrive by sailboat, since he had publicized the fact that he was coming to take up his appointment by sailing across the Atlantic. We hadn't known about his trip, but we got there a week before he did and thereby unintentionally stole his limelight.

The Norwegians couldn't have been nicer to us. We were greeted at the yacht club by a Captain Paulsen, who told us it was too late to change our money at the bank and very kindly offered to lend us two hundred kroner for our evening's expenses. We gladly accepted, and set off by taxi to the telegraph office to cable home that we had arrived. For the first and last time, we tried using German to explain what we wanted, since we couldn't speak Norwegian and assumed that German was similar enough to be understood, but the driver wouldn't move until we explained in sign language. We were very much embarrassed that we had temporarily forgotten the terrible time that Norway had had under German occupation during the war.

On our return, Mentz von Erpecom, commodore of the Bergen Yacht Club, and his handsome wife Birgit asked us to their house for a bath and drinks. Their enormous tub had its hot water supplied by a "geyser," or gas heater, directly above it. The Norwegians pronounced it "geezer," as did the British, and it made for a certain amount of amusement. When Dave Seeley's turn came, he seemed to be taking a very long time, and I went up to find him sound asleep in the enormous tub, with a seraphic smile on his bearded face.

One of the problems for us in Norway was that, because it was light all night and parties seemed to go on forever, we were never sure quite what we were being invited for. "Drinks" seemed to include whole meals, and we never knew when we were supposed to leave. The Norwegians were so friendly, however, that if we were gauche, they never seemed to notice.

On the passage over, Sally had lost an inlay in one of her molars, and I had replaced it with a very temporary filling. We were therefore delighted to find that the vice-commodore of the yacht club, Dr. Grevstad, was a dentist. He replaced my repair with a proper filling, though he warned that it might need more extensive work when we got home. Later, at a party in his house, his sister played the piano for us. It turned out that she was the top pianist of Norway. When she saw how much we enjoyed her playing, she invited us to her house the next day and had a recital just for us. (She even had her piano especially tuned.) She played a program of Bach, preceded by coffee and homemade chocolate cake—a thoroughly delightful afternoon! Mentz took us on a shopping tour of his department store Cloverhuset, and we were invited for a visit on the square-rigged training ship anchored directly behind us, the *Statsraad Lehmkuhl.* We had coffee and cookies in her beautifully paneled after-cabin. Later we asked her captain and his officers on board *Loki,* but conditions were more crowded there and we could hardly get the whole group down below at once. Again and again, wherever we went that summer, we were asked ashore to parties, to visit yachts, and even aboard a Colin Archer-designed sailing Coast Guard vessel. It was a wonderfully heartwarming experience.

Sailing on the west coast of Norway was a revelation. There were fantastically beautiful fjords, steep sided and green in the early summer, with rivers, perhaps better described as waterfalls, rushing down the mountain slopes and through very steeply tilted, emerald fields to the water's edge. There were tiny farms along the edge of many of the fjords, and wherever we sailed, the farmers ran down to the water's edge when they saw the American flag to wave and welcome us, frequently asking how things were in Brooklyn. The fjords alternated with passages so narrow it seemed impossible to sail through them, but the charts were beautifully clear and completely reliable. Where the passages were too narrow to print soundings in them, they showed black lines through, with a sounding at one end of the line showing the minimum safe depth. The sides of some of the passages were so steep that we could pick branches off trees as we sailed by.

There were harbors everywhere, and some were really tiny. One was so small that we dropped *Loki*'s anchor outside, sailed on in, and rounded up to tie her stern to a tree. When it was time to leave the next morning, we slipped the stern line, pulled ourselves out to the anchor, and set sail while she still had forward way.

Many harbors were almost completely landlocked, with entrances only a few feet wider than *Loki*'s beam. One of these was Rasvaag, which is surrounded by islands with a passage about twenty-five feet wide between them. The approach was along a steep cliff with surf beating at the bottom of it. This kind of a situation can be tricky for a boat with no power, since a cliff usually lifts the wind, and the seas can still push a boat onto the rocks at its base. If it wasn't too rough, of course, we could always tow *Loki* with a dinghy—but not against any significant sea, only across or down it. This time we managed to keep the breeze. At anchor in Rasvaag, three boatloads of young, blond, blue-eyed Norwegians ranging in age from about three to twelve years old came alongside. We invited them aboard and gave them chocolate. None of them admitted to speaking a word of English, but they stayed most of the afternoon, charming us and obviously fascinated by us. Whenever we looked out the companionway or even out the porthole in the head, there were hordes of cheerful faces watching and grinning at us.

We gradually worked our way down the coast, encountering one gale that kept us holed up in harbor for a day. We then had an all-night sail around Lindesnes to Kristiansand, and then on to Arendal.

Bob Loomis had left us earlier at Tananger to visit friends in England, so Sally, Dave, and I sailed *Loki* to Arendal, where a Norwegian friend of Sally's brother found us a fourth crew member for the trip to England. Peter Frøhstrup was on his way to study in Scotland and was brave enough to try this free transportation to England, although he had had very little sailing experience. I think he later wished he had chosen more conventional transportation.

For the first five days, we slogged against head winds and head seas that were just the wrong size for *Loki*. It was rough enough so that she pounded hard, and I worried a good deal about the possibility of breaking some of her ribs as she slammed into it.

Visitors at Rasvaag, Norway

When we got to Cowes, we found she had worked enough to crack all the putty in the seams of her planking forward of the mast, but her ribs were intact. Peter was seasick a good part of the way, but gamely stood his watches even though he couldn't eat much. An added complication was the very heavy traffic of fishing boats and steamers that we had on the way. Once Sally counted fourteen steamers in sight at one time. Another night, I left Peter to steer while I went below to make coffee. When I came back on deck, I found him tacking between two steamers approaching each other at a normal passing distance—with us in between. I'm sure neither of them knew we were there.

The last night and day, the wind eased off and faired, so we were even able to set the spinnaker for a while as we sailed by Dover's famous white chalk cliffs, with the French coast visible across the Channel. It was really exciting to see these places we had all read about so many times—the Royal Sovereign Light Vessel, Beachy Head, the North Foreland—now real and visible, not just names in a book anymore.

We put Peter ashore at Newhaven and sailed on toward the Isle of Wight, passing the Owers Lightship in the dark and sailing west-northwest toward the Nab Light. There was a very bright flickering light behind the Nab that wasn't on our chart. It had us really puzzled. We later found it was a flare from an oil refinery near Southampton, but it was very confusing that night, since it was the brightest thing we could see. Finally, after sorting this out, i.e., deciding to ignore it, I asked Sally which side to pass the Nab tower on. She replied that the water was good on both sides. Very luckily, we left it to port, because, as we later found out, there was a row of steel pilings between the Nab and the shore that we would have hit if we had gone on the other side of it. *Loki* might easily have been sunk if we had. The pilings were part of a submarine barrier built during the war, but still didn't appear on our chart. Maybe the British were still hiding them from the Germans. Safely by that hazard, we picked up a mooring outside the harbor at Cowes at four in the morning, having logged 857 miles in order to sail the 600-mile port-to-port distance from Arendal.

The harbor master woke us early, and suggested that we move into the "Trot" after we cleared customs. We wondered what a trot could possibly be. Certainly not the forbidden English translation of Caesar or Cicero that British schoolboys call by the same name. Nor could it be a brief gut problem. You can't tie a boat up to either of these. It turned out to be a series of mooring buoys in the harbor. Between two of these, one could tie up with a bowline to the buoy ahead and a stern line to the one behind. Six or eight boats could lie abreast between two of them, but very good fenders were needed, as it could get really rough in the harbor, which is wide open to the north. We hoisted the quarantine flag, customs came right out, and as soon as we were cleared we sailed in under jib and jigger and tied up to the Trot not far from another American yacht, *Carina,* owned by Dick Nye.

We looked eagerly around at the harbor, already crowded with the cream of British ocean racers gathered for the Cowes Week races and festivities. For years we had read about the Isle of Wight, with its legendary yacht clubs and racing traditions, and we were eager to explore it all. Now our solitary cruising was over, and we had to settle down to serious preparation for the Fastnet, England's blue-ribbon ocean race.

7

Once we settled on the Trot, we relaxed after our passage from Norway and had begun the usual clean-up by putting everything movable out on deck to dry, when a rowboat came alongside and Bobby Lowein introduced himself. He told us that Errol Bruce (with whom we had been corresponding about being allowed in the Fastnet Race) had asked him to see if there was anything he could do for us. We asked him aboard, and he turned out to be a real charmer, as well as one of the top English ocean racing skippers and owner of the Class III *Rum Runner*. Our rating put us in that same class, so we saw a lot of him in the days to come and became very good friends.

Sally and I moved ashore to the Gloster Hotel that evening. Sally's diary said she "hated to leave *Loki* and the nice secure world she represented, but a wonderful hot bath and a shampoo felt very good, and the big comfortable double bed felt sinfully luxurious."

The next day, I decided to pay a visit to the fabulous sailor, author, and yacht designer Uffa Fox, who was a friend and sailing companion of the Duke of Edinburgh, the Queen's consort, later to become Prince Philip. Someone ashore pointed out Uffa's house sitting on piles next to the water. Between the piles there were several beached dinghies, with a man working on one of them. He said Uffa was in the house above and to go on up. I found him on the top floor in blue serge trousers held up by suspenders ("braces" in England) and no shirt, bleeding from a head wound into the sink. I said hello and asked if he'd like me to sew up his scalp wound. He replied, "Who the hell are you?" I explained that I was an M.D. just arrived on a small yacht from the United States via Norway. He told me that his own doctor was on the way, and when I asked what had happened he answered, "A great bloody lump of concrate fell off me house and landed on me head." The bleeding soon stopped, and Uffa took me for a tour of the house, including his drafting office and a living room where three champagne bottles stood in a close line on the floor, with a knife and a fork balanced across their empty necks. Uffa explained that they were a wicket, and that he and friends had been playing cricket the night before. Several large spots on the wall were the result of using apples for balls, and these "good hits" had been made protecting the wicket. Such was my introduction to one of England's greatest and most eccentric yachtsmen. Uffa was reputed to have ridden his horse into a pub after several drinks and then into an apple tree after several more, receiving another head wound. He was also said to have an ex-wife, an ex-mistress, and a current mistress all living on the Isle of Wight at the same time. If the Duke of Edinburgh had had to run for office, he might not have been able to afford a friend like Uffa!

There are some very plush upper-crust yacht clubs at Cowes, such as the Royal Yacht Squadron, where women are not allowed, although Sally and I did have dinner there one night in solitary splendor with an Irish host. I think he'd probably had enough to drink during the afternoon so that he found it rather intriguing to break the rules. He carefully explained that although women, and particularly wives, were not allowed in the club itself, there was an annex behind it for the mistresses of members. Presumably this all went on in an earlier era. At the other end of the spectrum was the Island Sailing Club. It stood at the water's edge, with a long concrete ramp (a "hard" in England) and a launch to serve the fleet in the harbor. Davey soon found out why they pulled their dinghies up on the hard, rather than tying them alongside. With a twelve-foot tide, you came back to find your dink either hanging in the air by its painter, or made fast underwater so you had to swim for it. Davey had to cut the painter on ours, rather than diving, when he came back to find it tied four feet under the surface of the very cold water.

Everyone tended to show up at the Island Sailing Club in the afternoon, and even though they had been racing dinghies, most men were in proper yachting jackets. They even raced in them. Here we met Major Atkinson, who was about eighty years old and locally known as "Atkey." He had been everywhere and done practically everything that was exciting and sporting, including solo climbing in the Himalayas. He was currently sailing on the equally antique *Zoraida,* belonging to one of the Ratseys of the famous sailmaking family. He adopted Sally, found she liked dry sherry, and was always on hand to ply her with Tio Pepe. Later, after the Fastnet Race was over and we were about to sail *Loki* up the Thames to London to ship her home, he decided that since our crew had departed, he'd better come along to keep us out of trouble. He arrived with a bottle of Tio Pepe and a bouquet of flowers for Sally. It was great to have him on board—we not only enjoyed his company, but as we got partway up the Thames we found we were missing a chart to the very harbor where we wanted to spend the night. Atkey said he thought he could pilot us in. I asked when he'd last been there, and he replied, "I think it was 1914 or 1915." His memory was excellent: he could and did pilot us in very successfully.

Another interesting inhabitant of the Island Sailing Club was a local surgeon who wore what appeared to be a small lobster-pot buoy hanging out of his breast pocket. After a number of drinks, my curiosity overcame my manners and I asked him point-blank what the buoy was all about. He told me that, in keeping with the British tendency to celebrate Christmas Eve with bang-up parties, he returned from one in very good form and got into bed, only to find that it spun around him in a most nauseating manner. Realizing what was about to happen, he asked his wife to rush the chamber pot to him, and he upchucked into it. Too late, he realized that his false teeth were in the pot. His wife, not feeling too well either, ran to flush the potful down the john, impervious to his gummy pleas to wait because he had "loss his falsh teef." Knowing just what to do, he said, "Dear, wake up young George and tell him what's happened. Have him get the crab net, open the manhole in the garden, and fish for the teeth while you flush the loo." This was done and the teeth were recovered good as new. "When my friends heard about this," he continued, "they decided to prevent a recurrence, so they gave me this." And he pulled out the buoy with a set of false teeth attached.

A few days later, Sally and I were at a cocktail party at the Royal Thames Yacht Club when Bill Gray, one of Dick Nye's crew on *Carina,* came to tell me that young Dick had hurt his knee badly. I hurried out to *Carina* and found that Dick had dislocated his kneecap. I gave him a shot of morphine, told him I'd be back with a surgeon, and returned to the Sailing Club, where I found my lobster-pot friend at the bar as expected. I explained that I needed him to fix up young Dick. He agreed, but said, "First we'll have a drink." Then he needed another for the road (launch). When pressed to get going, he said okay, but we needed an anesthetist (pronounced "aneesthetist" locally). The anesthetist was at the bar too, but he also needed a drink before departure. When I finally got him away from the bar, he had to return to his office to get his chloroform-ether mixture and a mask. He then insisted on pausing for another drink before we got in the launch and set off for the Trot to examine young Dick.

We laid Dick on the cabin sole. The anesthetist backed into the head so he could cover Dick's nose with a mask and started dropping the chloroform-ether mixture on it. Just then a face appeared in the companionway in yachting coat and cap. "I say, old chap, could you let us out of the Trot? We're in the middle, you know, and must get back to Hamble tonight." I replied, "So sorry, but at the moment we're just aneesthetizing one of our crew members on the cabin sole." He answered, "Oh, I *am* so sorry, wouldn't have asked if I'd known, you know." By this time, the alcohol and chloroform-ether mixture had pretty well gotten to me and I replied in my best British accent, "Think nothing of it, old chap—we do it almost every night at home." He disappeared, but when he did, I noticed that Dick senior was standing at the bottom of the companionway ladder with a fat cigar glowing brightly in his mouth. Thoughts of ether explosions in which patients have been killed came to mind, and Dick was requested to get the hell up on deck. My surgeon friend then replaced young Dick's kneecap, and we figured, thanks again, I guess, to the booze and ether, that the easiest way to get him into the upper bunk was for one of us to take his feet and the other to take his hands and swing him one, two, three and into it. This was done with no further damage, and we all returned to our own occupations.

The next morning I was surprised, in view of the expert treatment I had provided for young Dick, to get another call from Dick senior asking if I would go up and look at the top of his mast, which had received some damage in a previous race. Still well hung over, I got in the bosun's chair and was cranked aloft to find the masthead itself split from the halyard sheave pin to the top of the mast on one side and horizontally through the pin on the other. By this time it was too near the start of the Fastnet Race to make repairs, and Dick, against my advice, decided to go with the mast as it was. By some miracle, the mast held up and young Dick's knee recovered in time for the race, so it all worked out satisfactorily.

Dick senior is a very cool character. During a later, very tough Fastnet Race, which, incidentally, she won, *Carina* opened up and, leaking badly, had to be pumped around the course. After tying up in Plymouth, he turned to his exhausted crew and said, "OK, boys, you can let her sink now!" How I envy him that remark.

We'd come to England primarily to race in the Fastnet, England's major ocean race, comparable to our Bermuda Race. It starts at Cowes and goes westward down the Channel, around Land's End, across the Irish Sea, around Fastnet Rock off the southern coast of Ireland, and returns to Plymouth, a bit over six hundred miles. It was begun at the suggestion of Weston Martyr, an English sailor and author who was also a great friend of Alfred Loomis, our Bob's father. It is run by the Royal Ocean Racing Club (RORC). Until that year, 1953, smaller boats were not allowed in the Fastnet, but had a shorter race of their own, around Wolf Rock off the Isles of Scilly. We were very anxious to race in the main event, and had written to Adlard Coles, a well-known English racing man and author, to see if it couldn't be arranged. Alf Loomis had also written about us in *Yachting,* stressing that Adlard's *Cohoe* had been allowed to put on a false bow so as to be long enough for the Bermuda Race and suggesting that in all fairness *Loki* should be allowed in the Fastnet.

Adlard was anxious to return the favor and pointed out that since we had sailed across the Atlantic and the North Sea, it seemed quite obvious that *Loki* was capable of doing the Fastnet Race too, which made it hard for the RORC to refuse. In order to let us in, they simply opened the Fastnet to all the small Class III boats, and we were accepted with the rest of them. Ever since, the small boats have been allowed in the Fastnet, and this ultimately led to a lot of people getting drowned in the disastrous 1979 race, when the small boats took such a tragic beating in a gale in the Irish Sea. It is my belief, however, that the more healthy and ruggedly designed boats of *Loki*'s era and type would have fared far better in that gale than the modern small light-displacement IOR boats that suffered so badly.

We had thirteen days in Cowes to get *Loki* ready for the race. We had to get measured, buy and store provisions, check out charts, sails, and rigging, and do all the millions of things one does before an ocean race. It was a busy and fascinating time. Hauling *Loki* in the British manner was exciting in itself. Instead of using a cradle in the American fashion, she was simply grounded out on the marine railway car, and I was asked to stand on her starboard side to heel her against a rickety four-by-four upright. This was made fast with a piece of rotten, frayed line to one of her winches, and she was hauled jerkily up the railway while leaning against this weak support.

Apparently, at that time British owners didn't work on their boats in the yard. Since I worked on *Loki* along with the yardmen, I was occasionally mistaken for one of them and was asked by other owners to do various jobs on their boats, much to their embarrassment and my amusement when they found out I was an owner too.

We were told that we would be measured above the "chain bridge" up the Medina River. I was worried about getting under it: it was shown on the chart, but no height for it was given. A "chain bridge" turned out to be a ferry pulled across the river by chains laid on the bottom, so it was no threat to our masts! Getting measured involved, among other things, boring holes in *Loki*'s hull and deck to measure the thickness of the planking, all of which goes into the formula. My protests against this desecration were in vain, but the holes were small and easily plugged, so no harm was really done.

In the midst of all our preparations, we were invited to race on the British boat *Merry Dancer* around the Isle of Wight for the Brittania Cup. (*Loki* was too small to be allowed in.) By the time we'd tacked up to the Needles at the west end of the Solent, the genoa had been ripped on a pinrail around the mast and both jib-sheet winches had stripped their gears. After turning around the Needles, the course was a reach, which meant that we weren't so badly off without working winches. On the way home, by Nab Tower, *Carina* was passing us to weather and Mr. Spurrier, *Merry Dancer*'s owner and skipper, gave them a real British luff, so hard that they went about on the other tack with their genoa aback. After this we were very careful to pass far enough away from other boats so as not to be caught in the same trap with *Loki*.

Three days before the start of the Fastnet, Bob Loomis reappeared, much to our relief, since Sally and I had been working alone until then. The next day we took *Loki* in a local race with Bob, John Barney from *Carina*, and Martin Fleahy from an English boat called *Thalassa*. When we came back to Cowes in *Loon* almost thirty years later, we found no room next to the float at the marina, but *Thalassa* was tied up there, looking just as well as ever. One of the Fleahys, who still owned her, asked us to tie up alongside and invited us aboard for a drink—a very pleasant meeting after so many years.

There were numerous parties ashore, including one that ran constantly at the Island Sailing Club. One day the three British boats *Bloodhound*, *Foxhound*, and *Firebird* rafted together and gave a huge party that left a trail of empty champagne bottles floating downtide from them as we approached. This was a wing-ding in true British fashion. The three American yachts—*Carina*,

Howard Fuller's *Gesture,* and *Loki*—tied up together and gave a return party for the hospitable Britishers. Howard Fuller's wife was in a flap about the arrangements for this, especially about whether to ask Prince Philip (then still known as the Duke of Edinburgh), who was incognito at the time in Cowes to avoid complex protocol. She kept pestering Sally for advice, but got very little out of her, as Sally was too busy preparing for the Fastnet Race to worry about social matters. Finally, we asked the Royal Yacht Squadron, of which he was a member, rather than singling him out. At one point during the party, I noticed him standing alone in *Gesture*'s cockpit. I went over to introduce myself and asked him aboard *Loki,* where we gave him a drink, showed him the boat, and took him down below. He acted as a veritable magnet, with crowds of Britishers following him below into *Loki*'s by then very crowded cabin. He was relaxed and friendly in spite of, or perhaps because of, our informal American ways. It was a good thing he was incognito, because it was next to impossible to maintain proper respectful behavior in such a small cabin. British custom demanded that ladies dress at parties, even on board, in shore clothes, namely, dresses and high heels, and Sally conformed. This made it necessary for her to back down the companionway stairs in his presence—hardly the proper way to approach the royal family—but he took it all in stride.

Finally, the day before the race, Friday, August 7, the rest of our crew, Harvey Conover, George Clowes, and Bill Dodge, arrived from America. Sally and Bob and I were still a bit hung over from the party we held for the British the day before, but Dorothy Conover took over the cleaning and last-minute shopping. The rest of us pulled ourselves together to get the sails and other gear in shape. That night before the start, the Royal Ocean Racing Club was host at another cocktail party at the Corinthian Yacht Club. This is my idea of how not to get ready for a race, but the British seemed to take their drinking just as seriously as their ocean racing, and I must admit it didn't seem to slow them down at all.

The next morning we were under way early, stopping spinnakers and sailing around to let the new arrivals get the feel of *Loki* again.

After the two larger classes started at fifteen-minute intervals ahead of us in Class III, we crossed the line at ten-fifteen in a light easterly with our spinnaker set, either first over or very close to it. The breeze was light, and at that point in ocean racing history, the British didn't seem to work as hard or as effectively in light weather as they did in heavy. Americans seemed better trained in this kind of going, and since *Loki* had no power, we had lots of experience getting the best we could out of her in light weather. We soon drew away from our class and began to catch up with Class II, which had started fifteen minutes before us, and not long after were passing boats in that class and even catching up to and passing *Kailua,* who with the rest of Class I had started a half hour ahead of us. By four-thirty that afternoon, most of our own class was out of sight astern, and we were approaching Portland Bill, a long finger of land sticking out four miles into the Channel, with vicious tides running around the end of it. We got there at the end of the fair tide, and gradually worked our way around, close to shore, in the still-weak head current, leaving our competition to battle the growing head tide. The wind stayed light, and we were lucky again the next day in picking up the first of the fair tide around Land's End at the southwest corner of England. During the following night, as we were on the wind sailing toward Fastnet Rock, we had a tense moment when the breeze let us up enough to barely squeeze by to weather of Wolf Rock Light, only a very few feet from the rocks, rather than passing to leeward as planned. The rocks at the base of the light, wet with surf, were alternately invisible in the dark, then garishly lit by the sweeping beam. We were appallingly close. I was so full of adrenalin that it didn't seem very scary, but I think some of the others felt differently.

The wind stayed light and ahead all the way across the Irish Sea. One of the crew took a string of sun sights that disagreed with Sally's by about eight miles. I had to decide which set to believe and base our course on. Having sailed with Sally for so long, there wasn't much doubt in my mind that hers were the correct ones, and so it turned out when we got to the Fastnet Rock. We finally rounded the rock Wednesday morning, four days out

Loki, *soon after the start of the Fastnet Race* (PHOTO BY BEKEN OF COWES)

from Cowes, in an almost flat calm. By this time, we were up with many of the Class I boats—a very exciting place to find ourselves!

The rock was very impressive. It's far enough from the Irish coast to be open to the west and south, so the big Atlantic swells roll in to break against it without any interference. Even though there was almost no wind, the seas were crashing high up on the rock as we rounded, and there were enormous puffballs of foam downtide from it, extending out for a mile or more. The present lighthouse is the third one built on the rock. The other two were washed away.

We learned years later that *The Times* of London wrote at this point that *Loki* was clearly going to win the race. In a book written by Ian Dear called *Fastnet: The Story of a Great Ocean Race,* it appears that we were then ten hours ahead of *Favona,* the ultimate winner on corrected time. When we sailed by her so easily soon after the start, her crew had decided that the race was as good as won. *Favona* and *The Times* had both left out one important factor: luck. After a very fast spinnaker run for part of the way home, the wind dropped and left us flat becalmed for eighteen long hours on the night of Thursday the thirteenth and the morning of the fourteenth. Finally, that afternoon a very light breeze came in from ahead, and it took us two hours just to sail across Plymouth Harbor to the finish line. The committee told us that we were the first to finish in our class and fifteenth to finish in the fleet. We'd beaten a Class I boat, fifteen Class II boats, and all of our own class on elapsed time, but the smaller boats could still win because we had to give them time.

We sailed into Millbridge Dock, which is like a huge swimming pool. You enter at high tide through lock gates, which keep the high water in. We had just drifted in and tied up to the wall when I looked aloft at our racing pennant and saw that a good fair breeze had come up for the boats still in the race. Two of them got the wind they needed and finished before their time allowance ran out. We had to settle for third in our class after *Favona* and *Lothian,* the latter sailed by Francis Woodroff of Ratsey and Lapthorn. *Uomie* of Class II also beat us on corrected time. We had beaten the other American boats and the rest of the fleet, but we were brokenhearted not to win after coming so close. Such is the luck of ocean racing. We all tend to accept good luck as our due and discount it, but bad luck is something else again—something quite unfair that we really don't deserve. We'd had plenty of good luck at the beginning, and the gods of chance evened things up at the end—but they really didn't need to go that far!

Sally was so depressed that she went to Plymouth's largest department store and bought herself a very sexy dress and a pair of gold shoes to go with it, to raise her spirits for the prize-giving party that night at the Duke of Cromwell Hotel, but after the ceremonies we arrived back on board *Loki* gloomier than ever. We were about to go to bed when I noticed a steam switching engine quietly puffing away on the tracks near where *Loki* was tied up. I wandered over and started a conversation with the engineer, and asked him if he was going anywhere in the engine that night. He replied by asking if I'd like to go somewhere in it. I immediately said of course, and could I bring some of my crew? I went back to *Loki* and collected George, still dressed in white flannels, and Sally and Bob, also in party attire. We all climbed up into the cab. The engineer asked, "Would you like to droive 'er, sir?" He showed me the throttle, brake, and reversing lever, and we were off. The next two or three hours were spent with all of us taking turns driving her around the tracks near the dock, picking up "goods vans" (freight cars) and shunting them around to hitch them up with other vans. We had a great time, and when it was all over we invited the engineer and the fireman aboard for a drink. They weren't due to go off watch until six in the morning, so two of us girded our loins and stayed up the rest of the night to talk to them. These two men hated the nationalization of the railroads. They said they'd lost their pride in their own special lines, as well as losing seniority; the equipment was not as well maintained and supervisors' jobs were now political appointments rather than being awarded on merit—an interesting commentary on the socialization of industry for the supposed benefit of the workers.

With the Fastnet behind us, we set out to explore some of the coast of Devonshire before going home. The first day, we sailed to Salcombe, where we were invited aboard a Brixham trawler called *Provident.* I noticed two long four-by-four timbers lying on her deck, and asked what they were for. I was told that they were the ship's "legs." At first, I thought that mine were being pulled, but it turned out that they do function as legs to hold the ship upright when she grounds out at low tide. They are simply lashed to the sides of a ship with their ends on the bottom so that they keep her level.

Salcombe is a perfectly beautiful harbor. We went ashore and climbed up a steep hillside looking over the water and the enormous fields of barley blowing in the wind, with the rounded Devon hills in the distance. There were only one or two yachts in the harbor, but there was a whole fleet of sailing dinghies rigged as yawls, something I've never seen anywhere else.

The rest of our crew had to leave us at Salcombe, and Sally and I started out alone to cross the Channel for a rendezvous with our English friends on *Favona, Bloodhound,* and *Rum Runner* in a little French harbor called Lezardrieux. We planned to get to the French coast shortly before dawn so that we could get ourselves oriented with the French lights while it was still dark. Unfortunately, we never could get them all figured out before dawn obliterated them. The French weren't too precise about the timing of their lights, which made positive identification very difficult. In addition, we hadn't realized that, because of large variations in candlepower, some lights that were farther away looked brighter, and therefore seemed nearer, than closer but dimmer lights. All this left us unsure of our position. The tides on the Brittany shore can reach forty feet, and produce vicious currents on the very rocky and reef-strewn coast. We decided it was a lot wiser not to close with the French coast when we didn't know exactly where we were, especially without an engine to buck the tidal currents in case we found ourselves uptide from a reef. Reluctantly, we turned around and steered a course for England, ending up following a trawler sailing into Brixham Harbor. There were still quite a number of sailing trawlers using that harbor in 1953. Brixham is a wonderful old fishing village built on the sides of two steep hills, and it had and still has a friendly yacht club with a bath you can rent for a shilling. Later that day we were invited ashore to dinner by some new-made English friends and had a very pleasant evening. They even bought a bottle of bourbon for our cocktails that night.

A couple of days later, rounding Portland Bill on the way back to Cowes with a gale behind us, we were surfing down the following seas with a full main and a working jib and mizzen. On these wild rides, *Loki*'s bow wave reached back amidships and almost as high as the boom, and she left a foaming track down the face of the wave astern. We were outside the dangerous area of Portland Bill, according to the chart, where the very strong tidal currents over a rough bottom can cause dangerous seas, reputed to have sunk small steamers. In spite of the wind, it was warm and sunny. I was sitting in my shirt sleeves, steering, when I heard a roar behind me and a sea broke all over *Loki*'s deck, wetting the mizzen halfway up, filling the cockpit, and sloshing a good deal of water down the companionway into the cabin, where it even wet the log entry that Sally was writing up. I can still see the smudges, as I plagiarize her log to write this. It also sent the binnacle cover flying overboard. We took off the main, set the trysail in its place and proceeded at a more sedate pace. That must have been an isolated rogue sea—there were no more like it as we sailed on to reach Cowes at midnight. What a super sail that was!

A couple of days later, accompanied by Atkey, we set off for London and managed to carry a fair tide for eighteen hours up the Channel and into the Thames Estuary. This was possible because the tidal currents in the Channel run in on the flood around the south end of England, and around the northeast end of Scotland from the North Sea, to meet in midchannel. The same thing happens in reverse on the ebb. Furthermore, the point of meeting moves northeast upchannel during the flood, so if a boat is moving northeast with the flood, the point where the currents meet keeps moving ahead of it. If you happen to catch the meeting point at the change of tide, you will not only have carried a fair tide longer than the normal six and a quarter hours, but can pick up the northeast ebb there and continue with a fair tide. Quite a neat trick!

When we got up to Ramsgate, just southwest of the Thames Estuary, we decided not to stop for the night, since the tide was now flooding again. It carried us along as we sailed up the river through the wide estuary by the anti-aircraft forts on the Maplin Sands and on toward Sheerness. At about six-thirty that evening, Atkey piloted us into the Medway River, where we spent the night.

Sailing up the Thames the next day, the wind was light and ahead, and we had to tack all the way. This wasn't so bad when the tide was with us, but it was almost impossible against a head tide. Our progress was further complicated by the large number of steamers coming downriver. It was a very busy sail, but the steamers were friendly and no real problems arose, even where the river was very narrow before London.

We passed several of the lovely old Thames barges still working under sail. They were about seventy feet long, sailed by a man and a boy. Their masts are in tabernacles and can be quickly dropped down on deck. They are reputed to be able to sail up to a low bridge over a river, drop their masts, shoot under the bridge, then raise their masts again and go on sailing without losing steerage-way—a maneuver for very skillful sailors.

Our last port was a town called Erith a few miles below London. There was a local yacht club whose clubhouse was the beached hull of an eighty-year-old lightship. Apparently, the boatman there had been alerted by Brigadier Hope of the British Army to have a mooring ready for us. We were a day earlier than expected, so we anchored for the night and got the mooring the next day. The brigadier himself arrived, with his aide, at about two-thirty the next afternoon to invite me, as skipper of one of the Fastnet Race competitors, to a formal luncheon at the Royal Artillery Mess in Greenwich. They got there at high tide, so I was able to meet them at the catwalk in the dink and ferry them out to *Loki* with no problem. The brigadier seemed pleased to have a few drinks on board, and one thing led to another so that by the time he was ready to go ashore, the tide had gone out and I couldn't get within a hundred yards of the catwalk. I had to land him and his aide on the slimy flats. The brigadier was totally undismayed. He stepped out, into mud almost up to his knees in his beautiful suntan uniform, turned and saluted, turned again and slogged his way up to the catwalk with his dignity perfectly intact.

I had gladly accepted the brigadier's invitation. The luncheon was a very formal affair indeed, preceded by several pink gins (a water glass full of warm gin colored with bitters), followed by several wines and excellent food, and then port, which progressed around the enormous table in a decanter transported on a silver carriage. A toast to the Queen was made, and then to the head of state of each guest's country, in the order of the length of time each had served. This was carefully explained to me in private beforehand so I wouldn't be offended by the fact that President Eisenhower was the last to be toasted. When all this was over, one could for the first time, without outraging tradition, smoke or go to the loo, whichever demanded attention first. Tradition means a lot to the British, as we found out when one of our crew upset them unwittingly at an earlier dinner by smoking before the toast to the Queen. I knew better this time, and avoided another gaffe.

It was time for me to get back to work, so we left *Loki* on the mooring in the Thames with the understanding that John Gray, one of *Carina*'s crew, would tow her up to the London dock with *Carina,* where they would both be put on board a steamer to be shipped back to the States. This went according to plan as far as *Loki* was concerned, but *Carina* suffered severe damage when a spreader holding the wires away from her hull broke as she was being lifted and let them squeeze her hull enough to split her house on both sides.

In New York, Dick Nye left the unloading of the two boats to me, but there wasn't a whole lot I could do about it. The job had been taken over by the stevedores, not the steamer's crew, and they didn't much care what happened to the boats. They started to pick up *Loki* with a prop still under her bow. This might have fractured her stem and some of her forward planking as she tipped forward in the sling. I did manage to stop them in time to prevent that, and no further damage was done to *Carina*. The two yachts were put overboard by the ship's crane and towed up to City Island to have their masts restepped at Kretzer's Yard.

8

One of the crew I'd signed on for the Block Island and Bermuda races of 1954 had to drop out because of an ulcer. Ed Raymond recommended Bill Thomson to take his place. Bill had just graduated from the University of Vermont. I asked him aboard and offered him a beer. He said he'd rather have milk if I had it. I said, "My God, you haven't got an ulcer too, have you?" He admitted that he had, but he came anyway and turned out to be one of the most valuable crew members we have ever had. He was always cheerful, no matter how tired and frustrated we were, and he had an unending supply of new bawdy stories. Sometimes he had us in such stitches that we couldn't see the compass. Bill pushes a boat as hard as anyone I've ever sailed with, but in spite of his presence, we only got a fifth out of twenty-seven in our class in the Block Island Race that year, and a fourth in class and fifth in the fleet in the Bermuda Race—nothing to be ashamed of, but we had been spoiled by earlier wins, and naturally hoped for something better.

That Bermuda Race was exceptional for the amount of excess paper that was supplied before the start. Pan Am airlines sent pages and pages of weather information; Woods Hole Oceanographic Institution sent a similar snowstorm about the position of the Gulf Stream; and even the North American Engine and Boat Manufacturers joined in. The unkindest cut of all was finding most of the Sunday edition of *The New York Times* wrapped around our Kenyon speedometer strut minutes before the start of our class. We noticed that we were going only about two knots, while the Kenyon showed us going ten, so the youngest of the crew, Jock Davis, jumped overboard and cleared it.

We had a rough passage through the Gulf Stream with a series of hard squalls. As one of these eased off, I went forward to replace the working jib we had shortened down to, and was dragging the unbagged genoa along the windward deck when it snagged on a deck block. I jerked hard, it came free, and at the same time *Loki* rolled out from under me and left me in the air upside down over the lifeline, which I managed to grab in passing. I remember wondering if I would knock myself out when I swung around and fetched up against the topsides. My head is hard, so I didn't do any damage. The helmsman yelled, "Man overboard," and the crew came boiling up on deck, where they stood in a line along the rail, leaving me no room to climb back on board. When they saw it wasn't a joke they were nice enough to give me a hand back on board, and even helped me set the genoa.

If the genoa had been bagged, it wouldn't have snagged, and I would have stayed on board. Neater than you like is apt to be regarded as "nasty-neat," but keeping things shipshape does pay off in safety and less fatigue in the long run.

There was so much paper to keep track of in *Loki*'s limited storage space, that by the time we reached Bermuda, Sally and I had lost the slip with our room reservation ashore written on it. She thought she'd recognize the place if she saw the name, so we hired a taxi and drove around town. This, too, failed to produce the desired result. Someone told us of a recently married couple who had a spare room right in town, which they would be glad to rent for a couple of days. We looked them up and found that he was a pleasant Bermudian of about fifty, recently married to a much younger English girl. They were glad to take us in and even offered us cocktails, which we happily accepted before going into town to have dinner with our crew. When we came back some hours later, we found the new bride outside the door of their house with a black eye and a bloody nose. It seems that an argument had arisen between the newlyweds, sometime after we left, and one thing led to another with drastic results. The injured bride had been taken in by a friend, but couldn't sleep. She was returning for her sleeping pills, and asked if we would sneak into her husband's room and extract them for her. Before I could say no, Sally said, "Sure," so we crept in to find her husband snoring loudly on his back in bed. We did find the pills and gave them to his wife, at which point I tried to persuade Sally to go back to the boat with me. Years before, I'd spent a winter on the then-famous traumatic shock team at Bellevue Hospital in New York, working in the emergency room and sometimes with psychotic Bellevue patients. I really didn't want to get involved with any more drunks, and particularly not with any more fights between drunken husbands and their wives. Sally, dead tired and with less experience in the seamy side of life, longed to spend one luxurious night in a real bed after a hot bath, and talked me out of leaving, so we undressed and crawled into bed. We were just going to sleep, when there was a loud crash followed by swearing from the next room. Our drunken host had fallen out of bed and was loudly wondering what had become of his wife. This time, I did manage to persuade Sally that, even though crowded, *Loki* might be more restful than staying here, so we snuck back to her for what was left of that short night.

Bill Thomson was about to get married after we got back to the States, and he had a very important date with Jane, his wife-to-be, two days after we expected to get home. We thought there was plenty of time for him to make it, but *Loki,* of course, had no power, and the return trip was very flat most of the way. It wasn't long before we realized that there was a real question of whether or not we were going to make it in time. We were also about to run out of milk and wondered how Bill's ulcer would stand up under this double threat. He was fretting, but stayed cheerful and kept chanting, "I'm coming, Jane, I'm coming." At one point when the log spinner was hanging straight down, Dick Nye came by on *Carina* and gave us a tow for almost eight hours. The next day it was still calm, and so hot that we plugged the scuppers and filled the cockpit with water to keep our feet cool. On the fourth day, we only did between two and four knots, even with the spinnaker up. It took us five and a half long days to get back, but Bill did just make his date with Jane. Later we went to their wedding, and I've never been to a happier or more cheerful one.

Later that summer, in the bight outside Cuttyhunk Pond, we met Marty Katenhorn in his lovely 45-foot schooner *Surprise*. She, too, was without power, and Marty's crew consisted of his wife, who was crippled by arthritis, and "the boy," who acted as cook and topsail man, going aloft to tack the topsail whenever the boat came about. The boy was over fifty and Marty was well into his seventies. I would have thought that a topsail schooner was quite a handful for such a crew, but they handled her with an ease and dispatch that was a delight to watch. *Surprise* was designed before World War I by McManus, the famous designer of Gloucester schooners, and was a real beauty. Marty told us that he'd paid $750 to have the hull and rig built, and the boatyard then let him hire one of their carpenters, who finished the boat off inside for another $700. It seems impossible, but this was before World War I, when everything was a whole lot cheaper than now.

In 1956, we both raced on *Mustang* in the Block Island and Bermuda races. Looking back, the most memorable thing about those events was the chance to sail with Rod. Each race with him was an education in itself. It was more than a little exciting to be racing on that beautiful, fast *Mustang*. We thought and talked a lot about the tactics of offshore ocean racing that trip—about how much more important boat speed is than keeping strictly to the rhumb line, and how, if you're a long way from the finish line, it pays to alter course to pick up speed, if you can, even if you have to sacrifice sailing the shortest distance. If the finish is still many miles away, and you're hard on the wind, it will probably pay to crack the sheets a bit, if you can gain significant speed that way, and it certainly doesn't pay to hold high to "put some money in the bank." The wind is likely to shift before you get to the finish line, and, in most cases, the boat that has sailed faster and gotten nearer will be in a better position than one that held high and went slower. Rod also emphasized the importance of tacking downwind. Even though you have to sail farther, you do it at a speed great enough to pay off in the end. Keep the boat going fast, *and* keep track of where you've been!

Mustang won second place in her class in the Bermuda Race.

Afterward, in Hamilton, there was an incident that seems funny now, but certainly didn't at the time.

I'd gone ashore to meet our daughter Marianna, who was to sail home with us. On the way back to *Mustang,* we stopped at the bar of the Royal Bermuda Yacht Club, where I had a planter's punch and she had a lemonade. This was to be the night of the postponed "Captain's Dinner" on *Mustang,* since it had been too rough on the way down to cook the magnificent steak that Rod had brought along for that occasion. We were all dressed in our finest, *Mustang* was moored near the Royal Bermuda Yacht Club, and many local Bermudians were out in their boats admiring *Mustang* and the other racers. Rod was below cooking the steak, and I was on deck with Stu Hotchkiss, Rod's old friend and navigator. We had been enjoying the scene in the harbor for a while, when I looked over and saw that Stu was upchucking over the side. A few minutes later, I began to feel nauseated too, but told myself that I was a physician and experienced enough not to get psychogenic nausea just because Stuart was sick. It soon became apparent that, psychogenic or not, disaster was going to hit me too. Neat to the last, I took off my coat and tie and folded them up and looked to see if there wasn't one side of *Mustang* unoccupied by admiring locals. There wasn't, so I decided at least to balance the show by leaning over the opposite side from Stuart.

Sally came up to find out what was keeping us on deck, and to let us know that dinner was ready. Both she and Marianna were taking on a ghastly hue also, but they struggled through dinner in spite of their nausea. I'm sure Rod felt disgusted by what he must have assumed were his drunken crew members.

In fact, about half of the fleet was decimated that night with the same complaint. When I got back to the lab in New Haven, I started doing some research, remembering that the lemonade and fruit juice for the planter's punch had been kept in grayish, plated metal pitchers on the bar. A little reading revealed that cadmium is occasionally used for such plating and is soluble in the acid of fruit juice. It is extremely toxic and is a very effective emetic. This was almost certainly the cause of so many people being sick that night.

Arthur Knapp, one of the most famous racing skippers of that era, raced with Rod on *Mustang* that year, and his daughter, Corlis, also sailed back from Bermuda with us. She was swimming in the Gulf Stream on the way home with Sally, Marianna, and Bobby Erskine while we were becalmed. Rod and I kept a shark watch. Before long we saw a fin approaching and gave the alarm. Bobby, the perfect gentleman, left the ladder for the ladies and shot up on deck without it. As we motored away in the calm, we looked astern and saw that the shark was about eight feet long and was chasing the log spinner. Rod pulled it aboard to keep him from biting it off, and the shark followed right up to the stern of *Mustang*. Rod put the spinner overboard a few more times to tease him and jerked it away just in time to keep him from grabbing it. The shark finally kept on going and bit *Mustang*'s propeller, which almost stopped the engine. Some people say that sharks are safe to swim with, but if one will bite a 45-foot boat, I'd rather not take the chance.

The Storm Trysail Block Island Race of 1957 was a fluky one, with light winds and lots of fog. Sailing back from Block Island toward Plum Gut at night in the fog, we had to anchor *Loki* twice so as not to lose ground in the strong head tide. When the breeze came in again, we ghosted through a group of boats that were still anchored, their crews apparently not realizing that the wind had come up enough so that they could buck the tide. Buried in the fog, someone on an anchored boat yelled at us not to run him down. Sally laughed, and we heard another voice say, "My God, that was a girl." It sounded as though he couldn't imagine anything as mortifying as being passed by a girl in thick fog.

With almost no visibility, we headed for the corner of the beach on the southeast end of Plum Island, taking continuous radio direction-finder bearings and distance-off measurements from Little Gull Lighthouse. This was a very useful trick before radar and Loran were available. It works because of the difference in the speed of radio and sound waves in air. Dividing the difference in seconds between the time of arrival of the radio signal and the sound of the synchronized foghorn by 5.5 gives a pretty accurate estimate of your distance from the foghorn in nautical miles. In this case, we managed to pick up the beach from about fifty feet away, where we expected it to be.

In spite of our efforts, we had to be content with a second in class to *White Water*. She was a sloop-rigged sister ship to *Loki*—one of the twelve boats Sparkman & Stephens had built in Germany to *Loki*'s plans. She was owned by John White, our ex-crew member, and we decided that if we had to be beaten, there was no one we would rather have do it than John, a very skillful sailor indeed.

After the race, we dropped in on a formal dance at the Stamford Yacht Club. Sally started dancing with Toby Tobin, who had joined our crew that year. Both of them were still in rather grubby sailing clothes, and a yacht club official came up to ask them to leave the dance floor. Toby was just then illustrating a point with a wide, sweeping gesture of his hand, the back of which happened to catch the officious offical in the face as he approached Toby from astern. This didn't make him change his mind about asking them to leave. We thought it was pretty stuffy. If they wanted to have a dance on the night of the Block Island Race finish, they should have been prepared to have some of the racing crews join in. In any case, we left, and since there was a Cruising Club rendezvous at Price's Bend the next day, we started off at about midnight to sail there. The wind finally pooped out completely at about four in the morning, so we anchored where we were, well offshore, and had a snooze before sailing on to join the rendezvous.

Toby turned out to be another terrific addition to our crew. He is a fine racing man and marlinspike sailor, well versed in things like splicing, whipping, and other skills that many young sailors have never learned. Unfortunately, I told Rod about his virtues when he asked me some time later. The result was that Toby was asked to race on *Columbia* when she defended the *America*'s Cup. He went on to race in other Twelves in other defenses, so we never got him back to race with us. It's flattering to have your crew shanghaied for the top competition, but it's also nice, when you find a really good one, to keep him!

This was the year of a transatlantic race to Santander in Spain, and Blunt White asked Sally and me to go on *White Mist.* This I was more than delighted to do, as I couldn't afford either the time or the money to take *Loki.* Sally decided she couldn't desert the children again for such a long time, so, sadly, she had to miss this one.

I reported on *White Mist* on a Thursday afternoon for the Off Soundings Race. Remembering our previous blunder of getting there a day late on *Loki,* I made sure to get there on time. I didn't know Blunt and Marion very well, but they asked me down below and gave me a beer and showed me where to put my sea bag and oilskins. Sitting with them in the main cabin, I noticed a picture of a very tough-looking girl in a slinky black-sequined evening dress on the bulkhead at the forward end of the cabin. I wondered who this could possibly be. I knew that Blunt and Marion had a daughter, but this was hardly what I'd expected. Well, mine was not to reason why, so I sat back and took a sip of my beer. When my eyes strayed to the bulkhead again, my God—the girl didn't have a stitch on. How come I missed that before? As I moved my head from side to side to dress and undress her, I noticed smiles and suppressed guffaws on Blunt's and Marion's faces. It turned out to be one of those photographs that changes, depending on the angle that you see it from. In my innocence, I'd never seen one just like that before. Blunt was one of the world's dedicated practical jokers.

One of Blunt's pet hates was Milton Berle, and at a party a guest tuned in to Berle on Blunt's TV set. Blunt turned off the set, but on coming back into the room was faced by Berle again. This time, he went upstairs, got his son Bill's .22 pistol, leaned over the upstairs banister and shot out the TV tube, thus eliminating Berle for that evening at least. Another year Blunt sailed in the Buenos Aires-to-Rio race. Marion flew down to Rio for the festivities. While she and Blunt stayed ashore after the race, some of the crew made the most of their absence by entertaining some of Rio's lovely and willing girls on *White Mist.* Marion was upset and asked Blunt to put a stop to the crew making "a regular whorehouse out of the boat." Blunt's answer was, "I don't see how that can be, Marion, the girls aren't getting paid."

Blunt was also a very serious and competent racing man—foresighted and careful. He asked me to check over *White Mist*'s rig in Newport two days before the start of the Transatlantic Race. I found that the fore-and-aft through bolt holding the tang tight to the head of the mainmast, which in turn was the point of attachment of the backstay and the forestay, had backed off almost all the way, allowing the tang to move sideways and twist. This had fatigued it and cracked it more than halfway through. Obviously, we couldn't sail to Spain with that, so Blunt called Merriman's, the marine hardware manufacturer near Boston, and got them organized to make a new one on the following day. We pulled the mast and took the old tang off for a pattern.

Early the next morning, Blunt and I took off, almost literally, in his supercharged Thunderbird. It was raining, and I drove, with Blunt in the passenger seat urging me to let her go and he'd pay for the tickets. We got to Merriman's in record time without being stopped by the cops, but it took so long to make the new tang that we only finished mounting it on the mast that evening, too late to restep it in the boat. This was finally done the next morning, the day the race started. In spite of the rush it all held up fine, but it's hardly the ideal way to start a transatlantic race.

We were over the line early at the start and had to come back and cross it again, losing about four minutes. With the excitement of trying to catch up with the rest of the fleet, nobody really planned how we were going to get past Nantucket and out to sea. Chick Larken, the navigator, and I began to worry fairly early, but with one thing and another, by the time we got to posing the question to Blunt, the decision had already been taken out of all our hands. It was too late to head up and go through Nantucket Sound, or to bear off and skirt the shoals south of Nantucket. At that point, either of those routes would have taken us out of our way and put us farther behind. So we passed close to the south side of the island and straight over the shoals that extend for many miles eastward toward the lightship. As evening came on, so did the fog. There are no buoys over the shoals where we had to cross, so it was, to say the least, an exciting night. *White Mist* was a centerboarder, and there were occasional yells to "Get the board up!" If she had been a full-keel boat, I think we simply wouldn't have made it over all those sandbars.

I found out later in the race that Blunt was starting an attack of prostatitis, and that he'd had one some time before the race. This can be a very debilitating disease, and Blunt was very sick with it for much of the race. I hadn't known about his previous episode, and so I hadn't consulted with his doctor, but Blunt took the medicine his doctor had prescribed, and I gave him a dose of what I thought he needed. It turned out that we were both giving him the same thing. There is a good safety margin in this drug, so all went well and he eventually recovered, but he had a very tough time before he did.

This brings up the point that it is important to check out the crew, as well as the boat, before a long offshore passage. Whoever is in charge of medical problems on board would do well to consult the crews' physicians if any problems are suspected. I should have done this, but didn't. As the Cold Duke in Thurber's *The Thirteen Clocks* said, "We all have faults, and mine is being wicked."

Several days out, running downwind with the spinnaker set, *White Mist* broached in an eighteen- or twenty-knot breeze and lay on her side with her main boom in the water, still going fast. Unfortunately, there was a vang, also acting as a preventer, rigged to the middle of the boom, and when the boom tripped in the water, it split horizontally down both sides for almost its full length. Vangs on old-fashioned boats with long booms, especially on centerboarders, should be rigged to the outboard end of the boom, not the middle. If the boom trips, the vang may break, but the boom won't. We got the mainsail down, sheeted the boom in and put it in the boom crotch, with the break supported by the main halyard. Chick and I, who were the most experienced carpenters on board, took time to plan the repair in detail.

I had brought several three-foot lengths of threaded bronze rods with nuts and washers, just in case we had spar problems. Blunt had oak wedges on board, with holes drilled in the thick end so they could be nailed in place, as well as galvanized wire and wire clamps. We drilled holes big enough to receive the threaded rods down through the track on top of the boom and out through the bottom, then pulled the break together with line and fastened it with the threaded rods cut to appropriate lengths. Then we cut up the bottom of one of the bunks in the main cabin for lumber to make splints. These were screwed on the sides of the boom over the splint, using every screw that we could find on board. Finally, every few feet, we wrapped lengths of the galvanized wire as tight as we could around the repaired boom, fastened them with the clips, tightened them up with the wedges, and fixed the wedges in place with nails. The ends of the wire were padded with Kotex, which Blunt had brought for this very purpose. This protected the sail and us from the sharp wire ends.

It took us about eight hours to make the ugly but strong repair and get the main up again. We had to lash the foot of the sail to the boom because the nuts on the threaded rods and the wires around the boom were in the way. During all this time, the boat was kept sailing under a genoa and mizzen.

Careful planning was a very important factor in the success of this repair. A job that's approached helter-skelter, with everyone putting in his two bits' worth, almost never gets done right. The repaired boom stood up perfectly for the rest of the race and even on the trip from Spain to England, where it finally got a more finished rejuvenation.

Our next major problem, some days later, was a low-pressure trough and gale that lasted for three days, well off the coast of Spain, with the trough oriented parallel to the European continent and perpendicular to our course. No matter which tack we chose, we seemed to be on the wrong one for the finish line. We were down to a double-reefed main, number-two jib, and jigger, when

White Mist's repaired boom

it became apparent that we had to replace the mainsail with the trysail. We got the main off, put the trysail on the track, and I started to hoist it up. I was stupidly wearing rubber gloves because of the rain and spray. My hand slipped off the winch handle, the brake on the reel winch failed, and I got a sharp rap on the back of the fingers of my left hand. I could feel a bone break, but it hadn't started to hurt, so I finished hoisting the trysail and started to go below to fix my finger. Blunt, not realizing anything had happened, asked me if I wasn't going to finish by trimming the trysail. So I went ahead and trimmed it and could feel the bones moving a bit in the break, but it still didn't hurt much. Then came my chance to get back at Blunt for his bulkhead picture. I said, "I've set your bloody trysail and trimmed it. Now do you mind if I go below and set my finger?" Then I pulled off the glove, which had a fair amount of blood in it, and pointed out that the break was compounded too. Blunt blanched. I went below and set the finger (badly, it's still crooked) and got Chick to give me an injection of antibiotic to prevent infection of the bone. In his enthusiasm, Chick broke the needle off in my butt. Fortunately, he was able to get it out with a pair of pliers. After this, I did my own injections. Blunt was now all contrite, and gave me a large scotch. He even let me sleep in that night. For years after that, he used to call me "my private physician" and say proudly to all and sundry, "Show him our finger, Doc!"

Beryl Markham, in her book *West with the Night,* says, "The essence of elephant-hunting is discomfort in such lavish proportions that only the wealthy can afford it." This might well be said of ocean racing. Bill Snaith, owner of *Figaro,* and our competition in this race, once compared it to standing in a cold shower, tearing up hundred-dollar bills. Compare it to what you will. I can vouch for the fact that in this gale it was wet, cold, frustrating, and exhausting on deck. Below it was wet, steamy, and sleepless, with the smell of unwashed bodies, yesterday's meals, and today's dirty socks. Yet none of us wanted to be anywhere but right there on *White Mist,* gale or no gale. Ocean racing, like heroin, is addictive.

In spite of our misadventures, we arrived off Cape Finisterre the morning of the finish as the sun rose, with Bill Snaith's slightly larger *Figaro* visible about a mile ahead. We gradually caught up with her, and I was given the honor of steering as we passed her by. We beat her to the finish line, but Dick Nye's *Carina* won the race overall; we were first in our class of three.

The next morning, Spanish reporters came on board to ask if we had any exciting stories of the race. When we tried to tell them about our heroic repair to the boom, they were totally uninterested. We didn't seem to have anything else to discuss, until I looked over the side and saw that the bumboat oarsman who had rowed them out had an obvious strabismus, i.e., his two eyes looked in very different directions. This reminded me of my "CCA eye," and I went below to get it.

My so-called Cruising Club eye needs a little explanation. There are many fascinating stories of exotic glass eyes with naked ladies instead of pupils, or simply red-and-white spirals designed to give a casual onlooker a sickening surprise. There are also reputed to be bloodshot glass eyes created to mimic the various stages of morning-after-itis in the good eyes of those who have overindulged

The Cuckolds, Maine

Isle au Haut, Maine

Rod Stephens reefing Mustang

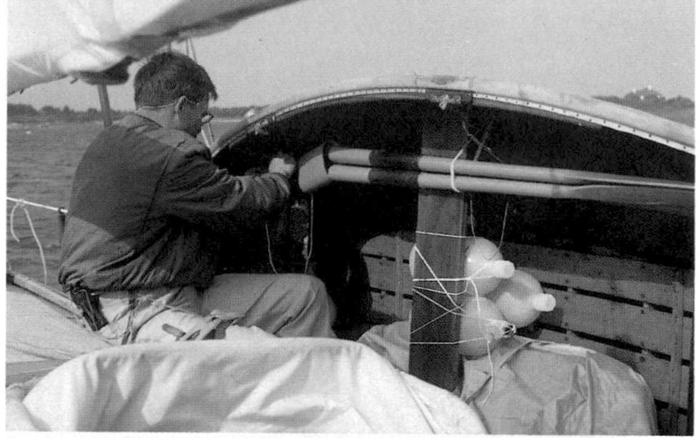

Bob Loomis stowing dinghy

Steering Loki

Sandy and Peter

Haugesund, Norway

Frenchboro, Maine

Young pilot whale

Minke whale close aboard

Salcombe, England

Sally taking noon sight

A dangerous tern of events

"Neptune"

The Eye (PHOTO BY W.E. TOBIN III)

Easterly wave

At sea

Kicker Rock (PHOTO BY GIFFORD PINCHOT III)

Land iguana (PHOTO BY GIFFORD PINCHOT III)

Angry frigate bird chick
(PHOTO BY GIFFORD PINCHOT III)

The harbor at Rikitea

Mangareva Peak

Rikitea church

Mangareva ridge and reef

Polynesian umbrellas

Motu, off Mangareva

Sally making bread

Dan the Merman (PHOTO BY GIFFORD PINCHOT III)

Outrigger canoe at Bora Bora

Loon *at Moorea*

Loon in the air

Loon and Tahitien

Thundersquall ahead (PHOTO BY RICHARD P. ANDERSON)

Raft rescue (PHOTO BY GIFFORD PINCHOT III)

Shallow water
in the Bahamas
(PHOTO BY ALAN FORSYTHE)

St. Croix sunset

the night before. I'd never seen any of these, but the idea appealed to my (warped?) sense of humor. One day, when I should have been paying attention to research, it occurred to me that I too could have such an eye without losing a good one of my own—all I needed was a contact lens. In those days, contacts were much larger, covering the whole white part of the eye as well as the cornea. Without further ado, I jumped on my bicycle and rode across town to an optical store and explained what I wanted. Opticians usually seemed to me a very stuffy and staid group, but as I explained what I wanted, smiles began to appear. One of them said he had a friend with a glass eye with a painted naked lady. I knew I had come to the right place.

I was told to wait until the contact lens man came back. When he did, he explained that contact lenses required a cast of the patient's eyeball and that a set cost two hundred dollars. This seemed pretty expensive for a joke, but on seeing my disappointment, he suggested trying a ready-made lens on the shelf. Spitting on his thumb, he wiped out the dusty interior of the lens, held open my eye, and popped it it. It was painful but not impossible, and he offered to paint in a small Cruising Club pennant—all for the princely sum of ten dollars. I quickly came back with the CCA book, showing a picture of the flag.

When my "eye" was finished, it could only be described as nauseatingly fantastic. The maker walked in with it in his own eye. It had a beautifully done pennant on a sort of a dead blue background that made it look as if the eye itself must have died some time before. Needless to say, I was delighted and added a bottle of scotch to the price. I've never had more fun for ten dollars and a bottle of booze.

It was a wild success in Spain, apparently appealing to some strange sense of humor like mine. Years earlier, it had been just as conspicuously an embarrassing disaster in England, when I wore it to a party at Cowes. Many of the British tried to avoid looking at me and at the same time pretended that nothing was amiss. This attitude prevented me from wearing it for the Duke of Edinburgh when one of his friends suggested it. Perhaps he would have liked it. Who knows? In any case, the Spanish reporters were intrigued, and the Santander paper had a picture of me on the front page with my evil eye in place, and a headline saying (in rough translation), "The eye of Dr. Pinchot is unique in the world."

I flew home from Spain with Bobby Simonette, who had raced over on Bill Snaith's *Figaro*. My shore clothes had never arrived in Spain, and the best I had was a pair of khaki pants with a torn back pocket, a knit shirt, and a yachting coat and necktie borrowed from Bobby. I've always preferred to fly with American pilots, so we booked passage on Pan Am. Much to my surprise, the Pan Am plane was flown by a completely Italian crew as far as the Azores. The Italian stewardesses thought Bobby and I were terrific, with our somewhat haphazard costumes, our new moustaches grown during the race, and a bloody bandage on my finger. They couldn't seem to get enough of us, and we enjoyed ourselves mightily. When we got to the Azores, an American crew took over, and the American stewardesses regarded us with deep suspicion and revulsion. We could hardly even get a drink from them.

In New York, the U.S. customs inspector asked me if I'd bought anything in Spain, and I assured her that I hadn't. She looked at my canvas sea bag, tied up with line, containing everything I had with me. I told her to go ahead and open it if she wanted to, but she'd have to tie it up again if she did, because of my broken finger. She didn't open it, but when I got home, Sally did, and found a long and somewhat decomposed object wrapped up in a bloody Spanish newspaper. I've often imagined how the conversation might have gone had the customs lady opened my sea bag.

She: "So, you didn't buy anything in Spain? What's this, then?"

Me: "Gee, I don't know, lady. Looks to me like what Shakespeare so delicately called a bull's pizzle. What do you think?"

Blunt and his crew of practical jokers had the last word after all.

9

In the spring of 1958 we found rot on *Loki*'s covering board, and some loose planking where it met her transom. This discovery really shook me. I thought we'd taken as good care of *Loki* as anyone could, but in spite of this she was in serious trouble.

Nichols Yard in Milford had a couple of good ship's carpenters who were able to work on *Loki* right away, so we took her there for repairs. Joel Singer, his father "Pappy," and I took off the toe rail and the covering board. Pappy was very small, a few inches over five feet tall. I don't think he weighed a hundred pounds. He was one of the most cheerful and enthusiastic people I have ever known. He loved his job and his invariable two beers with lunch, which in spite of his tiny size never interfered with his efficiency. While we were taking off the toe rail, Pappy would get himself all set with a screwdriver bit in his brace and get it engaged in the slot of one of the big number-16 screws there, then say, "Hold me down, Doc, hold me down!" So I'd put my hand on his back and lean on it while he took out the screw. Finally, we had *Loki* all repaired, but in the process we missed the Block Island Race.

That summer we kept *Loki* in a slip rented from Nichols. We couldn't get a mooring in the harbor, as it was just too crowded. The slip itself was a good deal shorter than *Loki* and pointed west, not quite into the prevailing southwest breeze. Getting in and out of it without power produced a lot of interesting boat handling.

The maneuver we developed to get in was to shoot upwind outside the slip with only the mainsail on, until we had almost lost headway. Then we dropped the sail and turned into our slip with the last of our forward motion. I stepped onto the end of the slip finger with a line from the midship chock and snubbed it there to stop her and make her fast in the slip. We used the midship chock because stopping a boat with a line from the bow pulls it into the dock, while a line rigged from amidships has much less of a tendency to turn the boat. Going out, we'd give her a good push backward with no sail on, steer her around so she was pointing more or less upwind, then hoist the mainsail and later the jib and mizzen, and tack out of the harbor.

In the Bermuda Race that year, we had in the crew Bill Thomson, his brother Bob, Ed Raymond, and, since *Mustang* wasn't going, Stu Hotchkiss. Even with this hotshot crew, we found ourselves in an almost impossible position a day out of Bermuda. The island was in a westerly wind and we were in a southeasterly, with an absolute no-man's-land of flat calm and a big and very confused sea in between. We had to get across into the westerly, which took several hours as we watched boats on the other side of the flat spot sail by and go out of sight ahead. We sat and slatted, tearing the very guts out of *Loki.* The seas were high and irregular, some almost conical. The jerking and slatting was horrible, but there wasn't anything we could do about it. When we finally got through to the breeze on the other side, we were all exhausted and had miserable headaches. Worse than that, *Loki* had started to leak from the punishment she was taking. By the time we had anchored in Bermuda, she was leaking so much I was afraid she might have spit out some caulking from her seams or suffered some other structural damage. I rented an aqualung and went down for a careful look, but couldn't find any obvious trouble. We decided to sail her home as she was, rather than hauling her out in Bermuda. She leaked quite a lot at first on the way, but by the time we got there, she had swelled up enough so that the leak had eased off, and we didn't have to do anything more about it.

Carleton Mitchell won the race overall for the second time running with *Finisterre* that year, while we were only slightly above the middle of our class. It was beginning to be obvious that there was more than just bad luck to explain our poor showing compared to *Finisterre.* She was exactly the same length overall as we were, a little longer on the waterline, and had a masthead rig. She sailed faster than *Loki* because of this, yet we had to give her something like three hours in this race because of the very advantageous treatment that centerboarders got under the CCA rating rule in those years. We were starting to think maybe it was time for a new boat, but very definitely did not want a centerboarder. The fact that centerboard boats broached comparatively easily, as I'd found out on the race to Spain the year before, was one thing I didn't like about them. They also had very little storage room for canned food in their shallow bilges, and because they were so shallow, it was easy for bilge water to get up into bunks and lockers. The centerboarders that I'd been on didn't sail too well upwind with a light breeze and leftover slop, which made them less than ideal for our kind of cruising without power. On the other hand, their very favorable rating made keelboats almost obsolete for serious racing at that time. In view of this dilemma, we decided to wait until the rating rules were changed, or until something more competitive in the way of keelboats turned up, before letting *Loki* go.

I had finally escaped my job in the Bacteriology Department at the Yale medical school and been offered one in the biology department of Johns Hopkins University. In the middle of August, we started our move to Maryland by sailing from Stonington, Connecticut, outside Long Island to the Delaware River entrance, and on to Chesapeake Bay through the Chesapeake and Delaware Canal, taking along our oldest son, Sandy, and our friends Camilla and Wister Meigs. One night, before reaching the Delaware River, we saw whole schools of fish outlined by the dim glow of phosphorescence. When we sailed into them, they shot off in all directions, leaving brilliant streaks of glowing silver light behind—a lovely sight.

We beat against light head winds alternating with rain squalls all down the New Jersey beach, and to no one's surprise the wind turned northerly to head us as we sailed up the Delaware. The wonderful names of the shoals in the river—Prissy Wicks, Somer, Overfalls, The Shears, Brandywine, The Lower Middle, Fourteen Foot Bank, Miah Maull, Joe Flogger, and finally Ship John—

cheered us on the hard beat up to the welcome protection of the Cohansey River, where we spent a peaceful night out of the current and traffic.

The next morning we sailed up to the C & D Canal and pushed *Loki* through it with an outboard on the Dyer dink we had towed with us. At the Chesapeake end of the canal, we were delighted again by the big green fields reaching to the water's edge. The whole bay was a cruising man's heaven, with its many rivers and creeks on the flat eastern shore, and the almost innumerable harbors, all lovely, and some so small they could only hold a couple of boats. The tall poplar and pine trees made a strikingly beautiful contrast to the low, level land, especially on hazy days when the depth of view was limited. In the fall, ducks and geese were often counted, not by the thousands, but by the acres of birds rafting on the water. The only fly in the ointment was the depth of the water. The Chesapeake Bay is the estuary of the Susquehanna River, and erosion from the many farms on both shores has made the water even shallower than it was in colonial times, when creeks and harbors now barely deep enough for *Loki*'s six-foot draft were ports for much bigger ships.

After several lovely weekend cruises to the eastern shore that fall, we laid the boat up at Gibson Island for the winter, where there was an excellent and very cheap yard run by the Lusby brothers. They stripped *Loki*'s hull of paint, planed her, and repainted her, all for $350. Furthermore, they had her finished and ready in the spring on the very day that I had asked for her.

In 1960 *Loki* was back in Connecticut. Lovely as the Chesapeake was in spring and fall, New England, and especially Maine, were more appealing in the heat of summer. Excerpts from Sally's log that year evoke some of the pleasures and problems of cruising without an engine.

> Sunday, July 10. Milford to Duck Island, Giff and Sally. 0830 under way after Giff made a trip to get more ice. Fancy exit maneuver consisted of rowing stern line out to free mooring buoy, pulling

her out of slip, reversing direction while fending off numerous powerboats, then hoisting mizzen, main, and #2 jib to tack out of the harbor. Wind E about 15 kts. Bright sunny day. Cool. Tacked slowly eastward vs. head tide. Changed to #2 genoa. 1700 decided to go into Duck Island for night. Dropped anchor 1800.

Monday, July 11. Duck Island to east. Up at 0615. Light westerly. Under way 0630. Just more than steerageway. Came to an imperceptible halt after 100 yards. Put out kedge anchor and got her off, only to stick again a short distance away. Decided this was the six-foot spot marked on the chart, but never before located. Spring ebb tide covered it with only 5½ feet [*Loki* drew 6]. Couldn't budge her, so, leaving main and mizzen set, went below for breakfast. 0800 floated off. Breeze still flat. Anchored again off east breakwater as we drifted in toward shore. Easterly zephyr in about 1100. Tacked towards east end of Sound, breeze varying between 1 and 10 kts. 1730 set up two-hour watches. 1830 at Cerberus Shoal buoy. Light fog in again. 2100 can hear the individual voices of Race Rock, Little Gull, Montauk, and Watch Hill all blowing. Beautiful yellow moon shining down on smooth haze-covered water. Peaceful night. 2300—no steerageway, and *Loki* insists on pointing west. Put dinghy over to pull her head around to the east, and felt much better that she at least pointed in the direction we wanted to go.

Tuesday, July 12. 0600 RDF fix places us one mile from where we were at 1830 last night. Soon after 0600, a breath of air came in from the west and *Loki* began to move. Tiny glassy ripples on the water, but leftover swells kept sails slatting. Changed wet #1 genoa, too heavy with water to draw, for

> drifter, and alternately winged it out and used it as a ballooner to fit the fickle breeze. Used RDF and distance-off to give us positions. Are holding our own against southerly set of current. Still thick. Speed 3–4 kts. 0900 Giff back on deck. Breakfast, sun burning off haze. 0945 at north buoy off Block Island. Course E ½ N for Buzzards Bay Lightship. Breeze freshened to 12–15 kts.—sailing a steady 6.5–7.3 kts. Point Judith, Brenton's Reef and Buzzards all blowing as we passed. Sailed into Quissett under jib and jigger picked up CCA mooring at 1830.

Our son Peter joined me and helped me sail on to Manchester, as Sally had other things she had to do. Rod appeared on *Mustang* and towed us through the Cape Cod Canal. We had a bang-up series of thundersqualls in Massachusetts Bay that kept Peter and me hopping, but Pete, then twelve years old, did a fine job of steering and handling sheets as I changed sails as needed. After a busy day, we sailed through the very narrow and crowded entrance to the tiny inner harbor at Manchester, where we were lucky to find a mooring. This was the first time there for me, and the high cliff on the west side lifted the breeze. We made it, but with adrenalin surging through my arteries. Sally arrived by train that evening, and we started off for Boothbay Harbor in Maine, getting a tow out of the channel by an outboard from the boatyard. We set up watches, with Sally and Peter on one and me on the other, and had a lovely fair breeze all that night, averaging about twelve miles in each three-hour watch. We picked up Seguin Island in the fog at three the next afternoon, and as we got to the Cuckolds near the entrance to Boothbay Harbor, the sun came out, and we tied up to *Mustang* by six-thirty that evening.

Then began a leisurely and delightful joint cruise with *Mustang*. We introduced them to Point Pleasant Gut one night, then sailed on the next morning to Pulpit Harbor on North Haven Island in Penobscot Bay, with a stop at Hurricane Island on the way—all in sparkling sunny weather and with the Camden hills sharp and blue in the distance. We explored Hurricane, and Rod showed us the delights of a freshwater swim in the abandoned quarry there. This was before Outward Bound rented the island, and at that time I didn't know it belonged to my cousin by marriage, Bill Gaston, who later gave it to his son Jimmy for a wedding present. Some wedding present. Cleaned and refreshed by our swim, we sailed back through Leadbetter Narrows and on to Pulpit Harbor, where the resident osprey was in her nest on top of the natural granite pillar at the entrance.

The next day, the breeze was so light we towed *Loki* out of the harbor with the dink, then found more wind outside and sailed on to meet Jane and Walter Page in their sloop *Barnswallow,* so named because Paul Hammond had her built in his barn and later trucked her to salt water to be launched. She's a very unusual boat, rigged to be sailed singlehanded, with halyards and even the anchor rode led to the cockpit, and with all sorts of ingenious gadgets on deck and below to make life easier. She is beautifully finished, and is still the apple of Walter's eye. After meeting them, we went back in company through Leadbetter Narrows to anchor in Long Cove, a narrow and beautiful harbor. From there we decided to make an expedition to the Basin after supper. The Basin is a rock-filled opening in Vinal Haven Island with a very narrow entrance, through which the tide really roars. It's possible to take a boat in at slack water, high tide, and even to anchor and spend the night, but it's so full of rocks and so high-sided and gloomy that we decided not to try it. We did get to see the Basin by foot that evening, though. A kindly resident showed us the way through the trees, and we got there with just time enough before sunset to have a quick look and rush back before dark. We didn't make it, and it was pitch black when we got back to the stone pier where we had left our drinks. Sally refused the offer of a flashlight, saying she could feel the edge of the dock with her feet. She might have, if she'd slowed down for it, but she walked right off the end and felt icy cold water instead.

From Long Cove we sailed around to North Haven and on

through the Fox Island Thoroughfare, across East Penobscot Bay and through the Deer Island Thoroughfare, with its warm, brown granite islands capped with spruce trees, finally ending up in Burnt Coat Harbor on the south side of Swans Island. We found Rod there, tied up to Crawford Failey in his new Dutch bouyer *De Vrowe Christina*. She was a thing of beauty, complete with brass-bound oak leeboards, fine teak carving everywhere, and a beautiful Dutch tile fireplace in her semicircular main saloon—and she was flying a hoist inviting us aboard for cocktails!

> July 27. Burnt Coat Harbor to Sommesville. Fresh S breeze, almost reefing weather. Sailed into Jericho Bay with NW current and strong puffy wind, then through narrow Orono passage between the brown granite sides of Swans Island and the small islands just north of it—Orono, Phinney, and Round, and over Bass Harbor Bar. Wind died almost completely in the Western Way. Breeze back hard. On to Southwest Harbor. Moored for lunch, hoisted main and sizzled through long fjordlike Sommes Sound to Sommesville. Peter brought binnacle cover to dazzling polish. Anchored. *Mustang* tied up alongside.

Rod and his crew went westward, while we had a lovely short cruise in what we think is the best of Maine, east of Schoodic, and also east of summer visitors, supermarkets, and crowded harbors. Accompanied by Sally's brother Fred and his wife, also named Sally, on their boat for part of the cruise, we stopped at Dyer Bay, the Cow Yard at Head Harbor, and Roque Island, owned then by Peabody Gardner, who welcomed sailors to anchor and swim off the island's mile-long crescent beach of fine white sand.

From Roque, we caught a fine northeast breeze, which took us all the way back to Northeast Harbor in one day under spinnaker.

The next day we had to wait for a breeze before getting under way at two in the afternoon. By four o'clock, we had only reached Bear Island, a quarter mile outside the harbor entrance, so we decided to return, and I towed *Loki* back to anchor for the night.

Thursday, Aug. 11. NE Harbor to Buck Harbor. Underway at 0800 before breakfast. Breeze very light from E. Drifted out with the tide into the Western Way. Anchored in head tide. Re-led the mizzen halyard around the backstay, whipped wire-to-rope splice on jib halyard where wires showing through. Lined silver drawer with sticky paper. Mount Desert looked lovely and greenish blue under cloudy sky. Gradually cleared and breeze in from SW. Weighed anchor 1300, sailed across Bass Harbor Bar in very light breeze, then began pickup race with 60-foot white yawl who came out of Bass Harbor. Race lasted all afternoon. She, named *Meridian,* hailing from Miami, set a mizzen staysail and we followed suit. She caught us off Casco Passage, where we suffered a maddening series of wind flukes which stopped us dead, but we wiggled out from under and caught the new breeze first. Went through the number two jib, the drifter, and the genoa, with lightning-quick sail changes by Giff. The breeze now came in fair and stronger, and they gained steadily on us going across Jericho Bay and into Eggemoggin Reach, where they gradually passed us. In the Reach, the wind faired to let us set our spinnaker and we passed them again. Soon we heard cheers from astern and realized that her young crew had gotten permission to set theirs. Up it went, and she started to catch us again, but now the wind came more ahead and we shifted to the drifter. She soon had to strike her spinnaker, which took them much too long. We both eased along with a dying breeze and at 1830, still behind us, she started her engine and kindly offered us a tow, which we refused with thanks. Caught a light breeze that took us into Buck Harbor. Anchored at 2000. Delicious steak with artichoke hearts!

After a few more days of sailing in thick fog, short-tacking through narrow passages, changing jibs to suit wind and sea conditions, and keeping careful track of our position, we arrived in Boothbay, from where we began our trip home.

Monday Aug. 15. Boothbay westward. Flat, glassy calm. 1030 under way in a zephyr. Tacked slowly down bay while the haze came in and foghorns started up. By 1330 we had finally limped and staggered to the bell off the Cuckolds. Big swell kept sails slatting and frustrated any attempt to make *Loki* sail. Tacking through 120 degrees in order to move at all. 1530 light breeze from N., tacking down wind with big genoa on. Overcast, and have heard a few rumbles from distant thunderstorms, but nothing seems imminent.

Near Seguin a sudden very hard gust hit. (As they say in Chesapeake Bay, "The breeze began astirrin' and asighin' until it woke itself up, and then Cap'n, it began to blow!") A second, even stronger installment arrived. Ran her off so Giff could get the genoa off, but could hardly hold her down. She had her rail buried running off before it! Genoa got away from Giff when I let her up a little as I reached for the sheet. Genoa got under the bow and wouldn't budge, but the wind eased enough in lull to head up and rescue the genoa, unhurt. Both felt we had made a dangerous mistake in keeping the genoa on when we knew there were thundersqualls around and we were short-handed. Giff says he knows better now than to believe he can tell when a thundersquall is going to blow and when it isn't.

1730—still just a little beyond Seguin. Wind now ESE with #2 genoa on. Monhegan, the Cuckolds, Halfway Rock, Portland all blowing. Can hear the three grunts at the end of the diaphone blasts from Cape Elizabeth. Rumbling thunder and dark clouds over Portland.

Ate up the last of our fresh food for dinner to celebrate finally moving and getting out to sea—steak, onions, lima beans. Variable breeze stayed with us. We stood 2½ hour watches with both on for a half hour at the changes, for navigation and sail adjustments. Occasional rain with thunderstorms moving past us and ahead. The night was inky black and visibility very limited—no horizon, and it was hard to gauge oncoming squalls. Giff had one that blew 30, but with a downwind course this was no problem.

Tuesday, Aug 16, 0300. Squalls gone, wind NE at 15–25 knots. Sizzling along on course. Sky brighter.

The moon even came out for an hour before dawn, and when Giff came on deck we had a conference. Weather reports indicated continuing NE winds and good visibility for the next 24 hours. Decided to head around the Cape rather than going through the canal. Changed course to S. RDF bearing from Pollock Rip confirmed our E–W position.

Pollock Rip Channel, which we had to go through on our way outside the Cape, is a graveyard for ships. The current runs hard across it and sandbars along it shift. It is certainly no place to be in a small, engineless boat with anything but good visibility.

After sailing down the outside of the Cape, we came to the entrance in clear conditions, but it was blowing hard, so we shortened down to the jib and jigger. By the time we got around the bar to sail up to Chatham, several seams in the mizzen had ripped, so I set the trysail rather than reefing and hoisting the main. I took off the mizzen to sew it up while Sally tacked the boat up close to the beach near the entrance to Chatham Harbor. We anchored there in smooth water, in the lee of the land, despite a 20- to 30-knot northeaster, saving the bother of tacking up the narrow channel into the inner harbor. We'd done 160 miles in twenty-six hours, which we felt was good going.

The next day, we sailed her to Quissett, taking off downwind from our anchorage under bare poles while I stowed the anchor under the dink. We set the number-three genoa and the mizzen, and were soon going along at over seven knots. The breeze eased off as we passed Hyannis. We set the main and had no trouble bucking the strong head tide through Woods Hole into Buzzards Bay, but we did have a wet sail the rest of the way to Quissett, where we picked up a mooring early that afternoon.

Sally and I agreed that this was the best cruise we'd ever had in this country. Norway was more exciting, but this had good old friends, beautiful scenery in Maine, and what had become for us, by this time, the good fun of sailing in pea-soup fog. In earlier years I'd sometimes been scared in the fog (although I don't think Sally ever was). Now it was a hazard we could be pretty sure of handling. With a direction-finder, you always had the option, if you were really lost, of following a safe bearing to a harbor, or, since there aren't many RDF stations in Maine, of simply going offshore until the fog cleared. With modern electronic navigation it's all much easier, but, we are convinced, not nearly as much fun.

During that summer we had decided to build a bigger boat, as we hoped to make a long cruise to the South Pacific. When we got home, we found that my mother's health was deteriorating, so we stayed nearby and eventually sold *Loki* to a friend without ever going back to her in Quissett. I think this made the parting easier, but for all that it was very hard. Sally, *Loki,* and I had come of age together in the sailing world, thanks to the Norway cruise and our racing successes. We have never had as beautiful a boat again, or one we loved quite as much as *Loki.*

10

My mother died in the fall of 1960. She was easily the most extraordinary person I ever knew. She had tremendous personal warmth: people just naturally opened up to her, and told her their most intimate secrets and deepest desires, guilty or otherwise. Never having been to school, she was uninhibited by convention and routine and had a very active and unfettered imagination. Her formal education had been provided by governesses, but the informal part that she had acquired by reading and experience was very extensive indeed, particularly in poetry, architecture, history, and politics. She loved the last with a passion, and her incredible energy and interest in people made her very good at it. Pain and discomfort simply didn't interest her much, and she enjoyed the excitement of danger. After my father died, she continued to live in the house in Washington, where she was in contact with the politicos of the day. She maneuvered them with ease and skill. I didn't always see eye to eye with her, especially when she deplored my decision not to follow in my father's footsteps into politics (he had twice been governor of Pennsylvania), but we loved and respected each other very much.

Her death left us with many major problems: settling the estate, selling the Washington house, disposing of another one in Pennsylvania to the Forest Service, and dealing with the enormous accumulation of books, art, furniture, letters, and so on, that two generations of my family had collected.

In the midst of all this, we decided to replace *Loki* with a bigger boat that would be better adapted to taking us on the longer voyages we hoped to make. We went back to Rod and Olin Stephens for a yawl again, but this time we wanted a boat more like the New York 32s, with a cut-away forefoot and better light-weather performance than *Loki* had, as we also wanted to go on racing. Olin's boats of this era had a lower wetted surface than *Loki* or the 32s. Their keels were very short, with rudders placed well forward. This was good for speed and meant that they could be tacked quicker and with less loss of energy, but it also made them hard to steer downwind when it was blowing hard.

We decided to build in aluminum rather than fiberglass or wood. Rod didn't feel that glass had enough years of proven performance behind it, at that time, to be ideal for long offshore passages. Aluminum would be lighter and give us much more storage and tank capacity than wood, because the tanks could be made by welding off a section of the bilge, with the frames inside the tank, rather than built inside the frames as in a wooden boat.

We decided on 45.6′ LOA, 30.3′ WL, 6.9′ draft, with a beam of 11′. She was to carry 250 gallons of water, 150 of fuel, and 30 of alcohol for the stove. We gave her a diesel engine, since she seemed too big for me to tow with the dink, and we needed power in the Chesapeake and Delaware Canal to be legal.

We chose Jakobson's Shipyard in Oyster Bay, New York, to build her, as Jake had more experience than anyone else with aluminum at that time. We hoped to get some cruising and racing on her in the summer of 1961, but she wasn't finished until the fall. This was just as well, as it gave us the whole summer to deal with my family's houses and possessions, which were much too extensive for us to take on in our more limited lifestyle.

The building of *Loon* was not nearly so appealing to watch as *Loki*'s emergence from the wood shavings at Albert Lemos's yard. We missed the wonderful smells of pine and white oak, tar and cuprinol, and the great skills of the builders with their adzes, planes, chisels, saws, and slicks. There were no hot oak ribs to be pulled out of a steam box and bent inside ribbands, or mahogany planks to be cut on a big band saw and planed by hand to fit. Instead, *Loon*'s plating was cut out of quarter-inch-thick sheets with the screech of a power handsaw, and her aluminum frames were bent on an enormous steel plate. A welding gun's blinding light replaced bronze screws driven by hand with a brace and screwdriver bit. All in all, it was a much less romantic and appealing process than building a wooden boat, but it did produce a result with many advantages.

Aluminum is much less prone to leak than wood, is stronger for the same amount of weight, and it saves room inside. It is also free from rot. Aluminum boats give an amazing sense of strength and rigidity after you've been sailing a long time in a wooden boat. When I hoisted a jib on *Loki,* there was never an abrupt stop where I couldn't crank up another inch or so on the halyard. On *Loon,* when you get the jib up, you're there, and there isn't another click to be gotten on the winch, unless the jib itself has a stretchy luff.

On the negative side, one does have to take precautions against electrolysis on an aluminum boat. Dissimilar metals connected together, with salt water completing the circuit, act as a battery, and aluminum can be destroyed by contact with other metals like copper, bronze, and lead. To avoid this, *Loon*'s lead keel was electrically isolated from her aluminum hull. The bronze sea cocks were placed on Micarta washers, which in turn were bolted into the hull so that there was no electrical contact between the sea cocks and the hull itself.

We've also never thought that *Loon* was as pretty as *Loki,* partly because her design wasn't quite as pleasing to the eye, but also because painted aluminum simply isn't, to us at least, as appealing as painted wood and brightwork contrasting with each other. As has been so aptly stated so many times—a boat is a large collection of compromises.

We had a great party for *Loon*'s launching on September 10, 1961. There were many old friends there, both nautical and shorebound. We had sent out an invitation paraphrasing Marlowe's poem, "The Passionate Shepherd to his Love."

> Come lunch with me and launch my *Loon*
> and we will have the pleasure soon
> of seeing her slide down the ways
> at Jakobson's in Oyster Bays.

This produced some amusing replies, including Olin's:

> To lunch with you and launch your Loon
> Would be a pleasure and a boon
> But previous engagements yet
> Make necessary my regret.

Blunt and Marion White replied as follows:

> Whether Scaup or Strumpet, Dabchick or *C. galcialis*
> Blunt and Marion will be with you on September 10.

Our daughter Marianna broke the traditional bottle of champagne over *Loon*'s bow from on deck, and fortunately didn't swing as hard as her mother had many years before, so she stayed on board. Hank duPont had come on *Nor'easter,* his powerboat, and brought his enormous shiny brass cannon, which he filled with two old-fashioned glasses full of black powder. It went off with a roar, then *Loon* slid gracefully into the water. It was up to me to move her under power around to the float, so that everyone could come on board. This I did with some trepidation, not having handled a sailboat under power in twenty-four years. I took it slowly and all went well. Soon after this, Bill Thomson had me leaning over the edge of the dock looking for some blemish he said he'd discovered on her hull. The next thing I knew, I was swimming. It's the crew's prerogative to dunk the skipper after a successful race, but Bill apparently extended it to other momentous occasions. It was such a hot day that a swim felt fine anyway.

Loon was finally finished enough to go on a late cruise by September 23. She seemed enormous as we stowed things and cleaned up that first day, but soon shrank to the "normal" size boats get to be after you've sailed on them for a while. We sailed the next day in a flat calm. Sally's log said: "The motor worked like a charm all day, and we hated it. Both feeling strange in our beautiful new possession and missing *Loki*." On the second day, we had a really good breeze, and under jib and jigger *Loon* tore along with her lee rail in the water. We felt that she was much too tender and wondered if we had been short-changed on ballast, until we found out from the radio the next day that we had been in the tail end of a dying hurricane that had returned to the coast after a trip offshore. This made us feel a lot better. We continued east as far as Newport and brought her back to Jake's by way of

Loon (PHOTO BY MORRIS ROSENFELD)

Block Island, Hamburg Cove, and Port Jefferson for some final fitting-out. Then, with Bill Thomson and a friend of his, we sailed her down to the Chesapeake, where we had some fine weekend cruises.

I was checking over the hull with a voltmeter from inside one day, to make sure none of the sea cocks were grounded, and found to my horror that the lead keel was shorted to the aluminum. Thinking of all the stories I'd heard and read about the early aluminum boats being destroyed quickly by electrolysis, I immediately called Jake and made arrangements to have the keel dropped and reinsulated. It was now the middle of November, and we couldn't find anyone who was either free enough or fool enough to sail back with us in this cold weather, so Sally and I took off alone.

All went well until we got to the very bottom of New York harbor and anchored in Atlantic Highlands at midnight after an eighteen-hour run from Atlantic City. When we woke up the next morning, there was a freezing northeast gale, and it soon began to snow. I ate some coffee cake to fortify myself for the day, but it was overaged and quickly gave me staph food poisoning, with resulting vomiting and diarrhea. The vomiting I could have put up with, but the necessity of going below and getting in and out of all those oilskins every hour or so seemed just too much. At one point, I even thought I was having hallucinations. I'd seen a large black buoy with a radar reflector through the head porthole, and when I came on deck, I saw it again. Sally explained that she was having trouble getting her right-of-way from a ferryboat, and rather than alter her course after leaving a known position at the buoy, in the middle of a snowstorm with limited visibility, she elected to circle around it until the ferryboat passed. I hadn't noticed the circling in the head, or while I was putting my oilskins back on.

It was a hard day for both of us in the poor visibility with the wind dead ahead. Thanks to my infirmities, Sally was on deck steering almost all day. We were very glad indeed to tie up at City Island late that afternoon. The next day, we got to Jake's, and the problem with the keel was taken care of. The trouble had been that the lead keel was a little too big and had cut through the insulation when it was pulled up into the slot in the aluminum hull. Fortunately, *Loon* had suffered no damage from electrolysis, thanks to a good protective coat of priming paint on her bottom.

Loon did everything we could ask of her in the first two years of racing. She won her class in the Block Island Race in 1962 and 1963, winning respectively third and second overall in fleets of over a hundred boats each time. She also got a second in her class in the 1962 Bermuda Race, and had an overall win in 1963 in the Northern Ocean Racing Trophy, put up that year for the first time by the Stamford Yacht Club. This was for the best performance, to be selected from any four of seven available races, one of which had to be the Stamford Vineyard Race. The Block Island Race, in which we won our class, also counted as one of the seven. *Loon* only went in two other races, but she earned enough points in these to win. The first of these, the Essex Yacht Club's Sam Wetherall Trophy, was embarrassing, as I had given the Race Committee the wrong measurement certificate in confusion about which one applied to this race. The committee member I gave it to took one look and said, "If this is right, there's no point in anyone else going. It's over before it starts!" After we got this straightened out with the right certificate, things got even more embarrassing. Soon after the start, we got a good breeze that went over the heads of our competition. We were the biggest boat with the tallest rig, and we simply sailed away from all the other boats, proceeding around the course in solitary splendor. After we crossed the finish line, one of the committee asked how we made it so fast. Still embarrassed, I replied with an answer we had sometimes used on *Loki,* saying, "It was easy, we ran our engine!" Too late, I realized that this wasn't quite so funny, now that we had one! We knew of course that we hadn't cheated, but we weren't certain that the Race Committee, who didn't know us, was quite as sure as we were. All in all, this wasn't my favorite win.

Our next event, the Monhegan Race, started from Falmouth

Foreside near Portland, went around the Cape Porpoise whistle, then to the one off Manana Island, and back to Falmouth Foreside. There was a very fluky northerly that day, and I got a terrible start. By changing sails to fit every wind shift (and there seemed to be millions), we worked our way through the whole fleet and were first around the Cape Porpoise mark. Second would have been much better. We sailed into a flat spot just beyond the buoy, and watched and fumed as most of the fleet sailed around us. Eventually we got some wind too, but now it was less fluky, and it was harder to catch up to the others again. We ended up with a fourth on corrected time. In the Vineyard Race our third in class (thirteenth in the fleet) gave us enough points to beat Fred Lorentzen's Block Island 40, *Teal,* for the trophy.

We had always believed that bigger boats were easier to win with when we had *Loki,* and *Loon*'s performance seemed to bear this out. It really was indecently easy to do well with her those first two years, and it wasn't quite as much fun as when we were the young upstarts in a small and comparatively inexpensive boat. Now we were part of the establishment, and we couldn't escape the feeling that we had bought our way in. This didn't bother us for too long, however, since after the first two years the rule was changed again, and *Loon*'s rating wasn't quite so favorable anymore, and winning became a good deal harder.

As a cruising boat, *Loon* quickly proved herself. She was able, handy in close quarters, and fast on long offshore passages.

After the 1962 Bermuda Race, we sailed direct to Nova Scotia for a cruise in the Bras d'Or Lake, where it snowed one July day in Boulaceete Harbor. On the way home, we stopped at Machias Seal, a small island south of Grand Manan. Sally has had a passion for puffins ever since we met them on the transatlantic cruise in *Loki,* and Machias Seal is one of the few places where they still nest near our east coast. We saw a few of the chunky black-and-white birds, with their red bills and feet, flying around the island, but the rest of them had gone, as the breeding season was over. On an idyllic sail back to Maine—a light southerly over smooth sparkling water on a warm sunny day—I heard a sudden whoosh and looked up to see a whole whale in the air a boat length ahead of us. He fell back into the water with a mighty splash, and in a few seconds *Loon* was in the foam where he had landed. I called Sally on deck in time to see him jump again nearby off the starboard bow.

Then began an extraordinary demonstration that we could only interpret as friendly playfulness. For thirty minutes he swam alongside and under the bow, sometimes so close that I couldn't see him as I stood on the cockpit seat. It seemed impossible that we wouldn't hit him, but he was a master at letting us come very close without actual contact. Sally and I ended up on the foredeck with *Loon* steering herself as we looked down on him from seven or eight feet away, while he made repeated passes under *Loon*'s stem. If he had hit the bow with his flukes, he might have knocked us overboard, but it seemed clear that he wished us well and was simply showing off to a very appreciative audience. Luckily we have pictures to provide "corroborative detail to lend verisimilitude to an otherwise bald and unconvincing narrative," as Pooh-Bah put it in *The Mikado*.

The next summer, 1963, we sailed *Loon* back from the Chesapeake to Long Island Sound with an inexperienced crew, composed of one of our daughter's boy friends and our flying instructor, Bill Tyler. Halfway down the Delaware from the C & D Canal, at night, the wind came in very hard from dead ahead and *Loon*'s engine didn't have power enough to push her against the head sea in the shallow river. Sally and I had a choice—either both stay on deck all night, short-tacking down the river, or go back up with a fair breeze to find an at least partly protected anchorage. The nearest one was thirty miles back, behind Artificial Island. We did go back and anchored there in its lee, as close as we could get in the shallow water, but by this time it was blowing so hard that, even at anchor, *Loon* was taking green water over her bow at each sea. (Well, as near green as that muddy river can provide.) We put down our thirty-five-pound Danforth as a second anchor and rigged chafing gear on the rodes. I was cleaning up in the cockpit and thought I was alone on deck, when I wanted Sally for something.

When I called for her, Bill Tyler said she wasn't below, so I yelled at the top of my voice, but got no answer. I figured the only other place she could be was overboard, so in utter horror I started putting the horseshoe life preserver and its waterlight overboard in the vain hope that we might be able to find her before she was drowned. Sally then appeared and asked me what the hell I thought I was doing. What a fantastic relief! She had gone forward to check the anchor lines and couldn't hear me over the roar of the wind and sea. Visions of trying to find her that pitch-black night still haunt me.

We had another very foggy cruise in Maine that summer. At Jewell Island in Casco Bay, a couple of days before the Monhegan Race, it was so thick that we couldn't see the sides of the harbor, even though it's only three hundred feet wide. We had to get to Falmouth Foreside for the race, so we started off, using a trick that is valuable for fog navigation where there are strong tidal currents. The log says: "Stopped at each buoy to measure the strength and direction of the tide by keeping it close alongside and noticing the course and speed necessary to do so." With this information in hand it was easy to correct our courses for current by drawing vector triangles, and we found all of the many silent buoys on the way to Falmouth Foreside with no trouble.

After the Monhegan Race, we went back to the Chesapeake and had several late-fall weekend cruises there. On one of these, as we were sailing along at seven knots, Sally called from below that we were aground. This seemed unlikely to me, as the speedometer still indicated a good speed, but as I watched it gradually fell to zero. Sally was quite right. She had heard a sound like a kettle about to boil as *Loon*'s keel plowed through the very soft mud of the bottom. After that, when we heard *Loon* approaching the boil, we took evasive action!

By that time, we'd both earned our instrument ratings in airplanes and were having some excitement flying. Sally had even crash-landed in a snowstorm at LaGuardia because of wingtip turbulence left behind by a Constellation that landed about thirty seconds ahead of her. She had landed all right the first time, but her plane was uncontrollable on the ground because of the turbulence. When she tried to take off again and go around, she was in the downdraft and brushed the dyke alongside the runway, which eliminated her landing gear. She made a fine landing without it, but that finished the prop and didn't help the engine. She was very lucky (and so was I) that she didn't get killed. A commercial pilot who saw the whole affair wrote to tell me that she had done everything just right, and that he couldn't have done any better himself, given the leftover turbulence from the Connie. That was excitement aplenty for that day, but airplanes never gave us the sense of being totally dependent on ourselves that an ocean passage to a foreign land produces. Big Brother, in the form of the Federal Aviation Administration, always seems to be looking over your shoulder when you're flying—ready to get you out of a jam if necessary and possible, or, in its other role as policeman, to take your license away if you forget one of its myriad rules. We like flying, but felt that something was missing. We needed a bigger challenge.

It was obviously time for another long cruise, where you make your own rules, and where success or failure depends only on luck and your own skills. Sally was for a trip to the Mediterranean, while I was more interested in a return to the South Pacific. We soon found that the distances to Greece and to Tahiti were about equal from the East Coast, so we settled on the Pacific cruise. I was dying to go back, and to show her the places I had loved so much as a boy.

Now we were back in the throes of preparations again, and a Pacific cruise needed a lot more than one to Europe. Polynesia doesn't provide, even now, the ready access to spare parts that you find in Europe. (Don't worry about not being able to use money there, though. It's no longer possible to bargain with fishhooks.) So we spent our spare time that winter organizing spare parts (including engine spares, this time), charts, *Coast Pilots*, *Radio Navigation and Weather Aids,* getting visas and special permission at the Ecuadorian and French embassies to visit the Galápagos and Mangareva. (How I hate dealing with bureaucrats, who seem to take such pleasure in telling you that whatever it is you want to do, you can't.)

By way of special equipment, we had a second dinghy built that fit upside down over our old Grumman aluminum dink on top of the house, making it possible for two groups to go ashore at different times or to different destinations. We also took scuba gear and a compressor to pump up the tanks. These proved to be very useful for cleaning *Loon*'s bottom later on in the cruise, and were a safety factor in case of any underwater damage. We had a set of extra lower shrouds made up, with wooden ratlines seized to them, to let us climb up to the spreaders easily in order to con *Loon* through inadequately charted atolls. Many Pacific charts date from surveys a hundred or more years old and leave a lot to be desired in the way of accuracy. The safest way to handle this is to go aloft and estimate the water depth by color. With a little practice this can be very accurate, if you have the sun behind you, but it's totally useless with the sun ahead and reflecting off the water into your eyes. The navigational aids aren't always where the charts show them, either, so it's best to play safe and go aloft to make sure.

The auxiliary shrouds with ratlines weren't ideal because they weren't tight enough (the regular lowers took most of the strain), and the slack allowed you to swing back and forth pretty hard as *Loon* pitched in a head sea. I just barely missed being thrown off once, coming out of the lagoon at Raiatea. Mast steps (which we have now) would have been much better, but I didn't think of them then.

We probably should have replaced one of our nylon anchor rodes with chain for anchoring where there is coral. We didn't, and one rode got chafed a bit, but I'm still using it twenty years later, so it wasn't too bad a mistake. We did go down to check the anchor with an aqualung when there was a threat of serious chafe, though.

One of the things we didn't have to do was coat the food cans with plastic varnish to keep the labels intact and the cans from rusting, as we had done on *Loki*. *Loon*'s freedom from leaks made all the difference. I did make wooden floors for the bilge sections where cans were to be stored, to keep them free of any dampness from condensation. Dry supplies were stored in tightly closed plastic bags and stored in lockers.

Before we had finally decided on a Pacific cruise, we had already signed up a crew for the Bermuda Race. Among them was Dan Walker. We met him on *Mustang* on a memorable Block Island Race, when we bucked a thirty-knot westerly on the way home. *Mustang* was a wet boat and fast to windward, so we were all soaked and cold—and then it began to snow. I can still hear the plop of each soggy flake landing on my sou'wester. That was where the idea of a Pacific sail first arose, and when the time came to collect our crew for the Pacific trip, Dan was happy to sign on. He had recently gotten divorced and sold his book-publishing company, so he had nothing to keep him ashore. We couldn't have found a better man. Dan is a first-rate seaman, knows celestial navigation, and is more than capable with tools. Furthermore, he is always cheerful and easy to get on with, so he was a great addition to our crew. He raced with us to Bermuda, then flew home and met us again in Panama.

With *Loon* loaded down several inches below her normal waterline, we didn't distinguish ourselves in the Bermuda Race and could only hope that it was because we were overloaded. Our racing crew, except for "Mouse" Page, son of our old friends Jane and Walter, left us in Bermuda, and we signed on my boss Bill McElroy and Pippy Wick, son of Phil Wick, owner of *Mutiny II*.

I'd brought along *Loki*'s old hand-sewn mainsail for this cruise. It was a little short on the hoist and the foot, about equal to taking a small reef in *Loon*'s regular main, but it was fine for cruising in the trades and much more resistant to chafing than our Dacron sail. We bent it on, and *Loon* seemed to sail well with it. So, that accomplished, we headed out of Bermuda, bound for the Caribbean.

As we sailed away from Bermuda, we were lucky enough to see the square-rigged school ship *Danemark* close at hand tacking up to the finish line at the end of that year's Transatlantic Race. None of us had ever seen a square-rigger tack before, although most of us had read about it. It was fascinating to see her come up into the wind, backing her square sails. The jibs were then sheeted to windward to help the backed square sails on the foremast push her bow around. As she turned through the wind, her square sails were braced around to fill on the new tack, and finally the jibs followed suit. After she crossed the line, the midshipmen in their blue uniforms and white caps ran up the rigging and out on the yards to put in a "harbor furl" before going on to Hamilton.

Loon was put on course for the Sombrero Light in the Virgin Islands. Mac and I shared a watch, and Sally had Mouse and Pip on hers. This was Mac's first ocean passage, and in fact he had sailed very little at all. He learned quickly and was a great addition. He even supplied some amusement for the rest of us, as he really didn't quite believe that we were going to find a small island in the Caribbean by having Sally peer at the sun and stars through the sextant telescope. The two boys, on the other hand, were busy taking navigation lessons from her.

The only excitement we had on the way was a series of grade-A thundersqualls that appeared after a forecast for an "easterly wave." We were too new to the Caribbean at that point to know that easterly waves can turn into hurricanes, but we gradually got the idea as we listened to the attention paid them in the forecasts.

Six days out of Bermuda, we picked up the high hills of Virgin Gorda (the "Fat Virgin"), and Mac was much relieved. He sat in the cockpit with a happy grin on his face, puffing on his first cigar since Bermuda. We sailed into Trellis Bay in Tortola, anchored in the lee of Beef Island and went for a swim in the warm, clear water. Mouse returned very quickly with a dislocated shoulder. He and I had an unhappy ten minutes—his much longer than mine—getting it back in place. I was beginning to wonder what the next step would be, when to our mutual relief it popped back in again.

Then began a wonderful week of sailing and snorkeling in the Virgins. This included skin diving at Buck Island near St. Croix, where we took *Loon* inside the reef with only six inches separating her keel from the sand. We explored the reef with masks and fins, looking at fire and antler coral and fish in an exotic variety of shapes, colors, and sizes. Diving on a tropical coral reef is one of life's really great experiences. After swimming over the shallow coral, the sudden plunge of the reef edge into dark, deep water provides the added thrill of feeling that your underside is unprotected and that anything might rise up at you from below. Visions of big and hungry sharks kept coming to mind!

Mac had to leave us at St. Croix, and the four of us sailed on toward Panama, another thousand-mile hop. We had fair winds, often more than we wanted. We experimented with self-steering, using two jibs with their sheets rigged through snatch blocks to the tiller, with the main and mizzen furled. This worked beautifully running almost dead downwind, until it breezed up so much that one jib was enough. Once, with only a working jib, we logged 150 miles in twenty-four hours. The seas were very short and steep, which surprised us, since the wind and current were flowing steadily in the same direction, and the water was very deep—all conditions that generally produce much longer swells. Nevertheless, short and steep they were. It looked as if some of them must come aboard to join us in the cockpit, but apart from an occasional slop, they stayed where they belonged, and we stayed dry.

One day, as I was steering, we had a visit from a young sooty tern, who flew around *Loon* and over my head a few times before landing with a crunch on my straw hat. This was interesting and photogenic, but dangerous, as I was wearing him backward with his tail over my nose. To avoid disaster, I very gently reached up and took off my hat and the bird, setting both down on the deck beside me, with the tern still on the hat, totally unruffled. Another tern joined us that afternoon, and both spent the night on the forehatch. They left the next morning, well rested, we hoped, for the long flight to shore.

As we neared Panama it began to get really hot. One log comment said, "Eighty-nine degrees in the navigation drawer." I can only assume that this was because the thermometer was kept there, not because anyone had an interest in getting into the drawer with it.

After seven and half days of fairly rough going, but fortunately no hurricanes, we made our landfall early one morning and sailed on to anchor behind the mole at Cristobal, the Atlantic end of the canal. We were quickly boarded and cleared by customs, and then visited by our shipping agents, Fenton and Company. They were very helpful, as they knew what was available and where to get it, so they took care of our supply needs quickly and efficiently. I'm sure we were more bother to them than our small commissions were worth, but they treated us with friendly courtesy, just as if we were ordering thousands of dollars' worth of food and supplies.

The Panama Canal Authority insists on a pilot for all ship movements in their bailiwick, so we got one for the very short trip from our anchorage to the dock. He stood silently in the cockpit while I put *Loon* in her berth. Pilotage dues are figured according to tonnage in the canal, so after careful measurement of our "Cargo Space" by an official "Admeasurer," we were required to pay ten dollars for all pilotage, including a pilot and passage fee for our thirteen-hour transit of the canal the next day.

Our berth alongside the dock was in water covered in oil from spills during the fueling of big ships there. It soon began to rain, and the heavy black bunker oil spattered onto *Loon*'s white topsides. What a mess. Fenton then delivered three hundred pounds of ice, rather than the fifty we'd asked for, and a large wooden box of food that we'd ordered from S.S. Pierce in Boston. It was so beautifully packed that nothing was broken, and the wrappings kept everything dry in spite of the rain. In the crate there was a letter saying they had not sent the salt cod we had asked for, but had substituted canned codfish cakes instead, because, they said, salt cod goes bad in the tropics. How right they were! We noticed a terrible smell a few days later and traced it down to salt cod we brought with us from home. The demise of S.S. Pierce is a great loss to the cruising fraternity.

Our first night's sleep after the spell at sea wasn't exactly what we had looked forward to. There were two big ship arrivals near us that night, with the usual accompaniment of horns and whistles as the tugs pushed them into their berths. Then, at 5:00 AM instead of the expected 7:00 AM, Captain Rowe appeared to pilot us through the canal. We were just too late at the first lock to go through with our assigned lockmate, so we waited an hour for the next ship. It was the old army game of hurry up and wait.

We had been told that the best way for a small boat to go through the locks is "center locking," that is, with four lines to keep it in the middle of the lock while the water rushes in through seven-foot-diameter holes in the bottom, raising the level thirty feet in three minutes. As you can imagine, there's plenty of turbulence to bang a small boat around, and it could easily be badly damaged by hitting the sides of the lock. By piecing together docking lines and spinnaker sheets and using two anchor rodes, we had line enough for the four warps. Four men standing on the sides of the locks forty feet above us threw down heaving lines with monkey's fists at the ends, so skillfully that no one was hit and nothing was broken. We made fast our warps, and they were pulled up to bollards on the lock sides. As the water rose, we took up slack as *Loon* tried to surge from side to side, and managed to keep her in the middle and undamaged. After three hair-raising up locks, we motored into Gatun Lake and had a peaceful run of thirty miles through it. The first part was a pleasant trip around steep-sided volcanic islands, and then through the famous Culebra Cut, right through a small mountain, where the original diggers had so much trouble with landslides. There were still dredges working there when we went through. The peaceful down locks followed the lake and took us to Balboa.

During this long day, our pilot, Captain Rowe, regaled us with stories of his life at sea. (Before being appointed canal a pilot, an applicant has to have ten years' experience in command of ships at sea.) Then he told us about hunting in the Canal Zone, outlined the histories, intimate and otherwise, of his two marriages, and finally gave us a discourse on the national characteristics of the captains he had piloted through the canal. He didn't have much good to say about the Latins—too emotional and apt to scream and yell in a crisis. The Japanese he rather liked—cool up to a point, but when the chips were really down, apt to do a bit of yelling too. He cited the case of one Japanese ship he was piloting, explaining first that there is a forward current of about four knots running into the full down locks (the water flows out at the bottom). To be able to steer entering the lock, he had to have at least four knots' way through the water, and this meant a very brisk eight knots by the side of the lock. When almost in the lock in this ship, he ordered reverse, but got nothing. So he steered for the side of the lock and slowed the ship by the friction between her side and the cement of the lock side. This, he said, produced a lot of vocalization from the Japanese captain, and a large black mark in Captain Rowe's evaluation of him.

I asked about the chain that's raised to water level in front of each closed lock gate. Captain Rowe said that a big ship moving well would cut through this and the lock gate beyond like the proverbial hot knife through butter, with the result that the water in the full lock and the ship in it would be emptied into the lock below, causing a very interesting few minutes.

He went on to say that the British were the coolest of all, and therefore his favorites. He had a similar episode on a "Limey" ship going fast into a down lock. The English captain was leaning his forearms on the windscreen around the bridge, quietly smoking his pipe. When the order for full astern produced no response, Rowe turned to the captain and asked, "How long is it going to take your engineer to give me full astern?" The skipper answered without the slightest emotion, "No idea, Pilot. Never happened before," and went on smoking. This was our pilot's idea of the maximum *sang-froid,* and mine too, as we went into the down lock and right up to its head, with *Loon*'s very weak reverse power full on and a big ship coming up fast behind us. The Limey escaped disaster and so did we. We picked up a mooring at the Balboa Yacht Club at six-thirty that night, feeling that we'd certainly gotten ten dollars' worth from our pilot that day.

I had to fly back to New York to give a paper at a scientific meeting, after which I met our son Sandy, and we flew back to Panama together. Our agent Fenton had told me that I could save a Panama entry fee by telling the airline that I was a captain of a ship in transit in the canal. In truth, I was more interested in posing as a ship's captain for all and sundry than I was in saving the ten-dollar entry fee. The Pan Am ticket agent took the whole thing hard and gave me a difficult time, but by now I was determined and insisted. I guess she heard my remark to Sandy about "Miss Five-by-Five," because our baggage arrived in Panama the day after we did.

We all went to the Panama Hilton, Sally and I for a last night ashore and the rest of the crew for a last meal ashore. Since most of our baggage was somewhere in transit, Sally and I had almost nothing with us. This made the desk clerk suspicious, and he rudely demanded payment in advance for the room. As we walked away to the dining room, I made a joking remark about signing for the dinner and not paying for it—another mistake on my part, because at 2:00 AM that night, the bell captain woke us up and demanded immediate payment for our meal. I refused, and spent the rest of the night planning revenge. In the morning I went to see the hotel manager, told him what had happened, asked him to bring in his secretary so that I could dictate a letter telling Nicky Hilton what had happened in his hotel and demanded that the manager sign it too. This so shook him that he begged me to accept the dinner as a gesture of goodwill from the hotel, which I, with every appearance of reluctance, finally did. We got the free meal, as I had jokingly predicted, but it certainly wasn't worth that sleepless night.

11

With the new crew assembled, consisting of Sally, our son Sandy, Dan Walker, and Mouse Page, we were ready to take off on August 2 for the Galápagos and Polynesia. We were glad to go. The midsummer heat in Panama was oppressive, especially for those of us who had just come from the north. After a hot and hectic morning collecting last-minute supplies and a final trip into the yacht club to top off our water tanks, we set sail.

The distance from Panama to the Galápagos is 850 miles, and is usually a frustrating sail, with severe thunderstorms near the coast at the beginning followed by calms and head winds. We learned later that a singlehander, Jean Gau, had taken fifty-five weary days for the trip, but we were lucky this time and did it in a little over seven. When we had a choice of tacks, we kept to the east in the hope of being upwind for the southeasterly trades, which we expected to meet further along the coast. This strategy worked out well, and we were fortunate in having only one calm spell that lasted a few hours the second night out. After this, we had unusually good winds and reached the trades sooner than we expected.

Porpoises began appearing a couple of nights out of Panama. For some reason we hardly ever saw them in the daytime all during this Pacific cruise. In the bright phosphorescent waters, the columns of green light they left behind were eerie and beautiful as they shot alongside and played under the bow. We always felt that the friendly porpoises were a good omen, and we were glad every time they paid us a visit.

On the third day out, Sally's noon sight indicated that we should be thirty miles from a high rocky spire of an island called Malpelo, and sure enough, we saw it sticking up over the horizon a few minutes later. It looked so near, no more than ten miles at most, that I was convinced that Sally's sight must be wrong. I made the mistake of saying so, but it turned out she was right. It took us all afternoon to get it abeam. The air was so very clear that it made it look much closer.

Malpelo is a single rock jutting up out of the ocean a couple of hundred miles west of the Colombian coast, and there are more small rocky spikes around it. It was a threatening and somber sight as we passed it at dusk. We could see caves high up on the island, apparently carved by the surf when the island was lower or the water was higher. We wondered if there were skeletons or even treasure hidden there, and wished that we could stop and explore. Our chart showed only very occasional soundings, and there was no assurance that there might not be other rocks hidden under the surface, so, instead of exploring, we gave it a good berth and sailed on.

August 7 was Sally's birthday. This was to be her fiftieth. Many years before, when it had seemed quite impossible that we would ever get *that* old (after all, we were young, old age was for old people), I had promised her a team of hackney ponies for that momentous day. The fact that we were on a cruise made this a little difficult, but I had done the best I could when I was in New York by getting her a pair of seahorses in the form of a gold and sapphire pin, and this would have to do. Everyone but Sally had a sleepless night on the sixth as we prepared for the party the next day. Danny decided to bake a birthday cake—two layers, no less—in spite of the increasing head wind and sea that *Loon* was enthusiastically crashing into. He found the cake mix, and I was looking for the eggs, when Sally woke up, climbed out of her upper bunk, and told me in no uncertain terms to keep out of the egg drawer. There had been a catastrophe there before, when some eggs had been broken and later announced their problem with a very strong smell. We finally got Sally back in the sack without tipping her off.

In spite of the rough weather, Danny got the cake done, complete with icing. Sandy made a "Happy Birthday" inscription and a flower for the table out of pipe cleaners. We decorated the cabin with signal flags and wrapped presents madly while Sally slept, so it all came as a real surprise the next morning. The great party mood lasted all day and was celebrated with cocktails that evening. To add to the birthday pleasures, the sun came out, and Sally was able to get a position line after a couple of sunless days.

By this time, we had left the intense, muggy heat of Panama and started to feel really cold, even as we approached the Equator. The cause of this paradox is the Peru current, which flows north and west along the Pacific side of South America. The current is the result of the southeasterly trade wind, which blows the surface water away from the coast. Deep, cold water rises to replace it, lowering the surface temperature and chilling the air above it.

Deep ocean water all over the world is rich in the nutrients that plants need to grow, and when it reaches the surface and is exposed to sunlight, it stimulates the microscopic plants of the ocean, called phytoplankton, to very rapid growth. They were so dense in this area that the water was opaque and greenish rather than the clear blue we were used to in the tropics. Phytoplankton is the food, either directly or indirectly, of all animal life in the oceans, with only a few very specialized exceptions. As one would expect, this plankton "bloom" causes a dramatic increase in fish, bird, seal, and whale life. In fact, before it was disastrously overfished, this small area of the ocean produced one-fifth of the whole world's fish catch.

As I steered *Loon* through this rich green water, I thought about these upwelling areas in the ocean, which can grow far more animal protein per acre than the best that can be done on land. They could be of great significance to the millions of people suffering from inadequate animal protein in their diets—a condition tragically common in the tropics.

I wondered if there wasn't some way that deep water could be brought to the surface artificially, to create more productive areas and help solve this problem by growing an abundant supply of fish where it was most needed. Artificial upwelling could have great advantages over agriculture on land, which requires a great deal of input by man in the form of plowing, cultivation, and treatment with fertilizers, herbicides and pesticides. In contrast, the upwelling areas of the ocean go on being productive year after year without any input at all by man.

One reason natural upwelling is so very productive is that there is no lack of water for ocean plants, and this is very often what limits plant growth on land. Another is that the food chain is short in an upwelling area compared to the open ocean, where we harvest top predators such as tuna and swordfish many steps up the chain. A tuna, for instance, might have eaten small bonito, which had eaten mackerel, which had eaten tiny crustaceans such as copepods, which in turn ate phytoplankton. With each step in the chain there is a roughly 90 percent loss in energy. It would be much more efficient to promote plankton growth and then harvest fish that eat the plankton, without all the wasteful steps in between. In upwelling areas, the phytoplankton grow large enough to be eaten directly by fish such as anchovies, and this is one reason these areas are so very productive.

The big problem in trying to pump up deep water artificially on a small scale is that it would sink right back down again because it's colder, and thus heavier, than the warm water around it. It's only because the natural areas are so big that this doesn't happen there. Obviously, if we were to pump up cold water, we'd have to have something to put it in.

Once every four to ten years, the upwelling of cold, nutrient-rich deep water in this area is interfered with by a phenomenon called *El Niño,* named after the Christchild because it often occurs at Christmastime. When this happens, plankton growth is inhibited, and this shortage causes starvation or decreased growth and breeding failures all through the food chain. Fish, birds, seals, and whales are all affected. One of these episodes coincided with the overfishing of anchovies in the early 1970s, with the result that the anchovy fishery disappeared and has never really recovered.

El Niño is associated with a failure of the easterly trade winds, which are replaced by westerlies. It was once thought to be a phenomenon of only local significance, until a very severe one in 1982 and 1983 caused intense scientific interest and study. The studies revealed that the effects were widespread throughout the

Pacific. Replacement of the easterlies with westerlies meant that cold water never reached the mid-Pacific as it normally did. Air saturated with moisture over the abnormally warm water was blown to our west coast, where it brought torrential rains and caused floods and mud slides. In Australia the westerlies produced just the opposite effect—drought—because dry air over the deserts in central Australia was blown to the east coast, replacing the normally damp air.

As we neared the Galápagos, Sally wrote in the log: "Wearing duck pants (poplin over red flannel), two sweaters, quilted jacket, gloves, and oilskins. Never expected the Equator to be like this." Later, at home, I talked with a lady who had recently visted the Galápagos on a Lindblad cruise. She thought I must be crazy when I asked her if she had been cold when she was there. She said of course not—after all, the islands were right on the Equator! I didn't get very far in explaining why we had been so cold there, and she simply didn't believe my talk of *El Niño*.

The Galápagos Islands straddle the Equator, but we were bypassing the northern ones and had to cross the "line" to get to our destination, the port of entry on San Cristobal. Since I was the only one on board who had crossed it before, it was up to me to initiate the others into the ancient and honorable order of "shellbacks." This initiation is traditionally filled with all sorts of painful indignities for the recipients, but in this case I was so badly outnumbered that this seemed an unwise approach to take. Instead, I made up some doggerel about each of the crew's sins, put on a rope yarn beard and made a trident out of a fish spear. Then, in the guise of Neptune, I read the verses and had the crew kneel in turn to be knighted and given their certificates. To make the ceremony more impressive, and to provide photographic evidence of the crossing, Danny threw a coil of line out from the bow while I took movies of "crossing the line." It was never so visible in my previous crossings.

At noon on the seventh day out of Panama, we caught sight of a peak fine on our port bow, and by four that afternoon we were abeam of the northwest tip of Chatham Island, or San Cristobal as it is now called on the chart. As we approached, we could see how brown and barren the land was. A few cactus plants as big as stunted trees grew near the shore, but otherwise there was no green, no people, no animals, no movement, except for a few soaring seabirds. It was a bleak landscape, somber and forbidding.

We anchored in an open bay, the Bahia Stephens, which faces west, so we were in the lee of the island, in absolutely smooth water and close to a sandy beach. We sat on deck and watched the sunset turn the sky a smooth and even copper color over a trunky boxlike island to the west, called Kicker Rock. It was perfect peace to relax at anchor in the still night and to be able to sleep in, instead of going on watch after only a four-hour break. A few inquisitive sea lions came by to inspect us, and then went on about their business. The seabirds went home, and nothing moved in this strange other-worldly spot.

The next morning we motored out to Kicker Rock. Big for a rock, small for an island, it was even more impressive close to than it had appeared the night before. It rose almost straight up from the sea for over eight hundred feet, and then was cut off perfectly flat on top, presumably by many eons of surf. Furthermore, one end had been split from top to bottom, as if by a giant axe, leaving a straight-sided gap fifty to a hundred feet wide between the two pieces. As we approached, we could see two smaller gaps running right through the island but not reaching the top.

On the west side we found a more gradual slope to the water's edge, and the three other men launched the wooden dink and rowed ashore, where they were met by two sea lions who were quite indignant at being awakened so early in the day. The rocks were covered with enormous barnacles as much as three inches tall. Running over the rock and the barnacles were some very dressy blue and red crabs. Danny was just able to scramble up a steep cliff and throw down a line to help the other two climb up to where the going was easier.

They found nests of frigate birds, or man-o-war hawks, who make their living by stealing fish from the very aptly named boobies. The boobies are beautiful divers. They spot fish from a hundred feet in the air, fold their wings for a vertical dive through the air and knife into the water to make their catch. The frigate birds soar in the air above, chase the boobies and make them drop their fish, and then catch the fish before they hit the water. Boobies have much stronger-looking bills than the frigates, and I would think could easily kill the much more delicate frigates, but they meekly give up their catch instead. It has recently been found that boobies are also victimized ashore by a specialized kind of Galápagos finch with a very sharp bill, which sneaks up behind the boobies, makes a small cut in their skin, then drinks the blood that flows out—a sort of a vampire finch. Darwin didn't know about this evolutionary adaptation, but he did describe another finch that acts like a woodpecker, using a cactus spine to extract bugs from holes in cactus pads. It's no wonder Darwin found these islands so fascinating, with a distinct species of finch having evolved on each island.

The shore contingent found another intriguing thing about the Galápagos—the wild animals were "tame." The boobies and frigates on their nests allowed the crew to walk up and touch them. There weren't any carnivores on these islands until humans arrived, when rats and dogs came ashore, so the other land animals have evolved without fear of attack until very recently. The goats and cattle put on the islands by whalers for a food supply were hunted, though, and they are wild and very difficult to get close to. Danny took a Cruising Club pennant on its staff to "claim" this island for the club, with just about as much legal right as European "discoverers" had in claiming the New World for their kings.

After the shore party returned, Sally, Danny, and Sandy set off in the dink to explore the splits through the island and to take movies of *Loon* sailing through the biggest one. There were no soundings on the chart in the split, but it seemed so complete that it was hard to believe it stopped at the water, so Mouse and I started to sail through. Unfortunately, the high island blanketed the wind, and it was too far to shoot through. We had to start the motor, and with that we did get through with no problem. This was something I had wanted to do ever since the skipper of my father's schooner had bragged that he could sail her through, but to my great disappointment never did.

With the crew back on board, we sailed on to Wreck Bay, the port of entry on San Cristobal. This was a real frontier town with ten or twenty simple houses lined up along a sandy beach. There were two ships in the harbor, one a Japanese tuna boat, which we learned had three hundred tons of frozen tuna on board. No wonder the fishing wasn't as good as it was when I was there more than thirty years before! The other boat was a smaller trawler flying the British red ensign. Her skipper, who had an Australian accent and didn't appear to be totally sober, called out as we passed that he was sinking, but refused our offer of help. He didn't even want Danny to go down with an aqualung to try to find the source of the leak, which he said his pumps were adequate to handle. He was on a delivery trip to Australia, he told us later, when we met him ashore. With that casual attitude, I wonder if he ever made it.

Jutting out into the water was the same old rickety pier that I remembered from 1929. The town had grown, though, thanks to a few more houses, still without glass in their open windows, and a sign on the end house proclaiming that this was "Avenida Carlos Darwin." One of the houses, roofed, like most of them, with rusty corrugated iron, had a hand-lettered sign announcing that it contained "Radio International San Cristobal." The proprietor was a shirtless Indian who stood in front of his office with his hand resting on the back of one of the donkeys that wandered about. Somehow we put across our desire to send a message home. He agreed, and pointed to a partially functional typewriter. After bending a few keys so that they worked, we typed out the message. He said "OK" and started madly twirling the dials of his transmitter. I began to think that this was all a macho pose for our benefit, but when we came back later he indicated that the message had been sent, and we owed him three dollars. We gladly paid, still believing that the whole thing was probably a joke on us. Months later, much to our surprise, we found the message had been received intact by Sally's parents.

After this was accomplished, and I had made our formal entry with the local authorities, we stopped for a beer at one of the two open shacks on the beach selling this commodity. Using my almost nonexistent Spanish, picked up from Mexicans when I went to school in California, I got across to the proprietress, Carmelita, that we wanted some beer and something to eat. By this time, Sally, a far better linguist than any of the rest of us, had somehow absorbed enough Spanish to tell Carmelita that I had been there on the *Mary Pinchot* in 1929 and had just come back in *Loon*. This produced much rapid conversation, the gist of which was that Carmelita remembered the *Mary* very well, and was delighted to see me again.

After buying delicious oranges and avocados and again dealing with customs to retrieve our passports, we mailed letters home. We tried to get fresh water to fill our tanks, but found it wasn't available. Then Carmelita showed up again with a present for us—the thick skin from the foot of a Galápagos tortoise holding a bouquet of artificial flowers. In return we took Polaroid pictures of her and gave them to her, which seemed to please her very much. This simple present was very well received all through the Pacific this time, while on the *Mary*'s voyage, fishhooks and beads had been the winners.

By half past three that afternoon, all the shoreside jobs were finished. We set off for Barrington Island under sail, but it was too dark by the time we got there to make out where the harbor actually was. It was an uninhabited island, and of course there were no navigational aids, so we stood offshore and hove to for the night, dropping the main, trimming the working jib to weather, flattening the mizzen, and lashing the tiller to leeward. We took turns standing solo two-hour tricks on deck just to be sure we didn't drift into trouble with unknown currents. A log comment reads, "It was hard to see just where we were. At times we could see the dark loom of the island, but at others the sky was blacker and the island disappeared. Several times I was startled to hear a loud ripple followed by a snort close at hand, but soon realized it must be only a night-prowling and curious sea lion."

At daylight we were seven miles from the harbor entrance. We tacked back and sailed in to anchor over a pure white sand bottom in twenty feet, surrounded by a small group of very friendly and amusing sea lions. Several were touching noses in what looked like a casual kiss. Others swam around *Loon*, performing all sorts of loops and rolls, as well as playing with *Loon*'s anchor rode and jerking the dinghy around by the painter. One even found an empty beer can on the bottom (not dropped by us), and kept retrieving it and letting it sink again. They were so beautifully graceful in the water that we were entranced and watched them for a long time, until they went ashore to haul out on the beach.

There were two lovely white sand beaches at the head of the harbor, one covered with females and their pups asleep in the sun, and patrolled by an enormous bull sea lion who probably weighed a thousand pounds. He guarded his harem by barking continuously, but none of the ladies paid him the slightest attention. We landed in two dinks, and a few of the mothers and pups rushed down the beach into the water in apparent terror, then turned to watch us, as intrigued by us as we were by them. Danny found one young pup sound asleep and patted him for a minute or two before he woke up, looked around sleepily for another fifteen seconds, then gave every impression of being terrified. He rushed down the beach for twenty feet and turned again to stare back at Danny, by now far more curious than scared. Wherever we went on the beach, we had an admiring circle of seals staring at us. We waded (gingerly, since there were some small stingrays and four- to five-foot sharks near the beach too) and were again surrounded by sea lions in a circle fifteen to twenty feet from us. Sandy put on a black wetsuit and drew the large crowd even closer, his color being apparently far more acceptable.

The big bull ignored us as long as we didn't get too close. When we did, he lumbered after us, but he was slow on land. He wasn't completely harmless, however, since we found another smaller bull who had apparently been chased up the beach and had a big open wound in his chest. We guessed he had been caught by the big bull while trying to steal a cow. There didn't seem to be any way he could get back into the water past the patrolling harem owner, so Danny distracted the latter by letting him chase him far enough so that we could drive the wounded bull back into the water, where we hoped he would have a better chance of recovering.

Beyond the beach the island was composed of black lava. It had a few big cactus plants with central stalks like tree trunks and branches supporting thick pads covered with long thorns. There were some low scrubby bushes, but the whole landscape was dry and barren-looking. Walking was slow and difficult because of the rough lava footing, and most of us didn't press very far inland. We did manage to find a few of the big yellow land iguanas, three or four feet long, looking like midget dinosaurs, complete with a row of clawlike spines down their backs. They had been hunted for food and were wilder than the mockingbirds and hawk that came right up to us without fear. The iguanas jerked their heads up and down when we approached in a properly reptilian and archaic fashion.

Danny had long wanted a set of goat horns, and set off with our Springfield 30.06 to shoot one. Goats are a serious hazard to the iguanas and tortoises, because they eat the cactus pads at the base of the plants, so that the lizards and turtles can't reach them. The Ecuadorian government was trying to eradicate goats at that point, so we felt Danny was doing the right thing. He shot a billy, the only one he saw, and had to carry it about a mile and a half back to the beach, covering himself with a very goaty smell and blood in the process. But he got his horns. After cutting them off, we hung the goat over the stern, hoping to attract some sharks, as Dan also wanted very much to catch one of these. Much to my surprise, no sharks showed up. When we left Barrington for Academy Bay on Indefatigable Island, we sailed out towing the goat. The breeze was light and ahead, and the goat made tacking very difficult. We composed a telegram to be sent to Olin Stephens, saying that while *Loon* was excellent for racing and long-distance cruising, she was no damn good for towing goats. It just goes to show what happens to your mind after weeks at sea. We all thought this was hilariously funny, and laughed at it again and again. Ho,

Ho, Ho, no damn good for towing goats! Back to the drawing board, Olin!

Barrington is the island where the *Mary* went aground and damaged her rudder so badly that we had to jury rig the steering gear and sail her back to Panama for repairs. Her professional skipper had put her aground once off the coast of Florida and twice in the Caribbean before his replacement caused the Barrington trouble, while on *Loon* we had sailed the same distance and had nothing go wrong. It's nice once in a while to be able to outdo the people you looked up to as the experts when you were young.

We got tired of towing the dead goat on the way back to Academy Bay on San Cristobal island, especially as he wasn't producing any sharks, so we cut him loose. Sally's log said, "Danny spent two hours on the foredeck scrubbing and rescrubbing his goat-bloodsoaked clothes in salt water and detergent. Apparently the goat still had quite a hold on us." I could sympathize, as I had shot a billy goat for food on the previous trip. I'd gutted it a good way from the beach, then carried and dragged it to the water. I too had smelled so powerfully of billy goat that I was almost sick on the way. We ate that goat, and he was still strong on the table after being cooked.

Later that day, we anchored in Academy Bay, just inside the Darwin Institute's *Beagle*—a gussied-up Cornish sailing vessel with a very fancy paint job. She'd been sailed out from England to provide transportation for research in the islands. Young Johnny Angemeyer rowed out to welcome us. The Angemeyers are a well-known family in the Galápagos and elsewhere, having accomplished all kinds of unusual things, from being one of the first families to establish a successful and permanent base here, to commercial fishing, violin playing, and even movie acting. We gave Johnny the mail we'd brought from Panama. Mail was routinely sent on visiting yachts, since there was no commercial transportation direct from Panama.

Later, a bearded young Englishman named Julian, who worked at the institute, came out in *Beagle*'s longboat and offered to let us use the washing machine there. This was very welcome, as we had a mammoth wash to do by this time. Three of us went ashore with him and set up a production line, running load after load in the tiny machine, washing in cold, brackish water, then wringing it fairly dry in a rickety hand wringer. When the wash was done, we rowed it back to *Loon* and hung as much of it as we could on lifelines and rigging. When we ran out of clothespins we tied it up with string. None of it dried too well because of the cold air and the brackish water we had washed it in, but at least it was clean.

Another pleasant young Englishman named Richard, who along with Julian had sailed *Beagle* out from England the previous year, showed us around the institute, which was set up to study and help preserve the islands and their flora and fauna. It included a pen full of enormous Galápagos tortoises, which, sadly, are getting rare now, partly because they have been killed for food and trophies, and partly because the goats compete with them for cactus pads—the favorite and main tortoise food.

The next morning, an American, Forrest Nelson, who lived in a cinderblock house on the opposite side of the bay from the Angemeyers, came to invite us for dinner that night.

Dan decided to have a day on board, while four of us went ashore to walk inland and explore. We had a fascinating trip, following the only road to the interior. It consisted of a narrow dirt track, just wide enough for one person or a horse, between lava outcroppings. Near the beach the land was powdery dry, with cactus and some dried-up scrub brush, but as we gained altitude toward the interior we began to find more dirt than rock on the trail, and the plants changed and became much greener. A few hundred feet higher, we were in lush vegetation composed of trees, brush, and flowers, and our feet were slogging along through slippery mud. Some miles inland we came out on a plain with houses built on stilts to keep them out of the mud. Pigs running loose provided garbage removal for the mestizo inhabitants. The path now led between huge avocado trees and carefully cropped coffee bushes, as well as banana plants and breadfruit trees.

Farther along we came to a European-looking house and met

its owner, Frau Horniman, who had lived and farmed there for much of her life. She invited us in for a delicious lunch, consisting of homemade noodle soup, braised beef (from the wild cattle that are hunted for meat), taro, sweet potatoes, avocados in the place of butter, and a wonderful fruit salad of oranges, bananas, mangoes, and king's fruit. All of this she raised herself, except for the wild beef. She lived a lonely existence, since her husband was ill and back in Norway. She was fluent in five languages and had educated her children so successfully that they had gone off to college in the United States and now had jobs elsewhere. She had one farm helper, an Ecuadorian, whom we had met on our way up, leading a pack train of donkeys loaded with food they had produced for sale down on the beach. We asked if there was anything we could give her. Her greatest desire was for books, so we collected some for her from our supply on *Loon*.

On the way home Sally fell and banged her knee, and I slipped and sprained my ankle, so we hobbled back together, arriving just before sunset. Richard and Julian had arrived for cocktails with Dan, so we joined them. Then Forrest Nelson came to remind us we were to have dinner with him, so we rowed ashore to continue our busy social life. We had a pleasant supper of mostly canned food with him, after which Sally and I stayed ashore in his tiny hotel for a less than luxurious night, shivering in slightly damp sheets, with one thin blanket making a feeble attempt to keep us warm.

There wasn't much shopping to be done at Academy Bay, but bartering worked fine. The next morning we swapped some canned meat, of which we had plenty, for Ecuadorian beer that Nelson had. It turned out to be delicious. He also let us have some of his precious rainwater to fill up our tanks and even offered to try to get a message back to the states via his short-wave radio. He was answered by an amateur in Maryland with a short-wave set in his car, who asked the usual question about where the transmission was from. When Forrest answered, the recipient said, in tones of astonishment, "You're WHERE?" I've always imagined him pulled off the road at a hot-dog stand on Route 40, getting a message from the Galápagos.

Our next stop was a semiprotected anchorage between Indefatigable and Seymour Island, now called Baltra. Nearby was a shallow bay surrounded by mangroves that was reputed to be full of sharks. Dan was still anxious to catch one, but when we went ashore the next morning no sharks appeared. Dan thought it would be a good place to give Sandy and Mouse some scuba lessons. This went well at first, but on swimming around a point of land, Dan came face to face with a large and inquisitive shark, who escorted him on his rush to the beach. After that there was no more scuba practice, and it was just as well. That afternoon the inlet was wall-to-wall sharks. It looked almost as if you could walk across the inlet dry-shod on their backs. I've never seen anything like that concentration, but they had their minds on other things. Not one would bite Dan's baited shark hook.

Sally baked some delicious bread and Sandy went off in the dink and caught an enormous snook and three small groupers. In spite of this success, the fishing wasn't nearly as good as it had been when I was there before. The grouper had been so thick and hungry then that they would bite at anything, including the outboard propeller. I tried to catch a golden grouper for the *Mary*'s scientific collection. These are fantastic fish, bright, true gold in color, not the reddish hue of normal goldfish. Once a golden was found, the problem was not getting him to bite a tuna jig lowered over the side, it was keeping the masses of normal gray grouper swarming up from the bottom from getting it first. In 1964, the number of grouper had been drastically reduced by very active fishing to supply dried fish (*bacalao*) to the Ecuadorian market on the mainland.

The next day it was time to push on, if we were to get to Tahiti in time for Mouse and Sandy to fly back to Harvard when it started that fall. It was already past the middle of August. We hated to leave the Galápagos after this very short stay and wished we could have taken several years to go from the East Coast to Tahiti, not the three and a half months we took.

We sailed north around Indefatigable and tacked north again along the east side of Albemarle, the biggest island in the group.

The visibility was fair as night came on, but with periods of *garua*, the local name for a light, misty drizzle.

As we sailed north and crossed the Equator again, the mist came down over the mountains. It was very dark and hard to tell how far offshore we actually were. When we turned west to set our course for our next island, Mangareva in the Tuomotu group, we had to pass between Albemarle and Roca Redunda, a small island to the north. With poor visibility, no navaids, and no lights on either island, this was interesting sailing. It became much more interesting when we began to hear surf ahead, because the chart didn't show any reason for it. The surveys these charts were based on were old and sketchy, with soundings very widely spaced, so reefs could have been missed. Our Fathometer readings showed no bottom, but as we got closer and closer to the noise, it was nervous work indeed. We kept going, hoping we would either get soundings or see the surf before we hit. It would have been a very poor place to lose *Loon*, even though we could easily have rowed ashore. There probably was no fresh water there, the going along the beach would be extremely difficult, with rough lava boulders and mangroves, and the only settlement was many miles away on the south shore. Fortunately, we didn't come to grief. The noise turned out to be a very active tide rip off the north point of the island. With a big sigh of relief, we set our course for Mangareva three thousand miles away and slightly south of west.

12

The passage to Mangareva was *Loon*'s fastest ever—3,000 miles in 17 days, 6 hours, for a straight-line-distance average of 7¼ knots. This was very good going in those days, before planing-cruising boats had been developed. In fact the *Mary* sailed the same distance, Galápagos to Marquesas, in only one day less, and she was 120 feet on the waterline as opposed to our 30. We had constant trades on this passage, varying from the port quarter to the beam, never dead aft and only ahead of the beam once, in a strong blow that lasted two and a half days and had us shortened down to jib and jigger trimmed flat, just able to lay the course. This was the dreaded Polynesian *maraamu,* or south wind. It blew up to force seven or eight and gave us a rough, wet ride. One night a big wave filled the cockpit and almost washed Sandy overboard.

After the blow, the weather got warmer as we sailed west. We had porpoises playing under the bow, occasional gannets, and pure white tropic birds, with beady black eyes and very long, spikelike tail feathers, to watch. There were often flying fish on deck in the morning, which we picked up and cooked for a delicious addition to breakfast. On the whole, it was sunny—an ideal tropical trade-wind passage, but with a little more wind than usual. With five of us on board we didn't have to work too hard, and we even got enough sleep. With a lovely Polynesian island to come at the end of the passage, who could possibly ask for anything more?

Mangareva is the easternmost of the Tuomotu group. The rest of the group consists of low atolls—rings of reef supporting low, sandy islands around central lagoons generally with passes on the leeward, or western sides. The islands themselves are scattered along the reef rather than continuous, and most are no more than seven or eight feet above high tide. The central lagoon in the largest may be sixty miles or more across. Mangareva, on the other hand, is not typical, since its reef doesn't make a complete ring and one part of the island is over twelve hundred feet high.

Darwin postulated that the atolls of the Pacific were the result of slow coral growth around the rims of extinct volcanos, which were sinking slowly enough so that the coral was able to grow as the land sank. His hypothesis was confirmed many years later by borings that revealed volcanic rock deep beneath the coral.

Although coral is primarily animal in nature and traps phytoplankton for food, it also has photosynthetic plant cells imbedded in the animal ones, which provide some of the energy that coral needs to live and grow. This explains why coral can't grow in deep water, where there isn't enough light to keep the plant cells happy. Apparently, Mangareva is a volcanic cone that was blown out on one side in an explosion, and this side was, and still is, just too deep to support coral—hence the partial reef.

Our U.S. hydrographic charts of the Pacific were based on old and inaccurate surveys, and showed areas called "vigias" with cheery notes saying that surf, or perhaps discolored water, had been seen in this region fifty or seventy-five years earlier. Points of land had been reported five or ten miles further east or west than shown, and there were warnings about the strong, unpredictable currents in this part of the Pacific. The hazards inherent in sailing around these islands are clear from the former name for the Tuomotus—the "Dangerous Archipelago." Eleven yachts and inter-island freighters were lost there in the year following our visit to Tahiti.

Routine determination of longitude requires correct time, and this wasn't available on shipboard many years ago, before radio time-ticks and accurate chronometers, so it isn't surprising that old surveys sometimes misplaced islands in east or west directions. Measurement of latitude doesn't require time, only a precise measurement of the sun's maximum altitude above the horizon, which can be determined by following the sun up with the sextant until it reaches its zenith. Latitude is more apt to be right than longitude in old surveys, but it pays to be wary of both, especially this far from help if anything does go wrong.

The opening into Rikitea's harbor through the reef at Mangareva is on the northwest side, and the reef there is totally submerged, about eight miles north of the high land. To play it safe, we planned our landfall ten miles north of the reef. The seventeenth night out of the Galápagos was a busy one. As we approached Mangareva, we had to be very sure of exactly where we were. Sally, Danny, and I all took numerous star sights. Sally got the best agreement (a series of three different position lines from three stars, giving the smallest triangle when plotted on the chart), so we used hers, and estimated that we should see the high peak of Mangareva off to the south at dawn.

As the first light started to show in the east, we looked hard to the south, but couldn't see anything but a dark cloud where we expected the land to be. We took another round of morning sites, which we were busy working out when Dan called up from below and asked what we were doing, since he could see the island loud and clear out a porthole. Sure enough, it had emerged from behind a large, fat rainsquall. Much relieved, we altered course to go in on a safe bearing, racing along on a broad reach under jib and jigger, which we had shortened down during the night so as not to overrun the island.

As we came close to the reef, I went aloft and stood on the spreaders to guide us into the harbor of Rikitea. It was unbelievably beautiful. I could see the bright blue bottom through seventy-five feet of water, and as we got into the shallows the blue was mottled with coral heads appearing light brown, while the white sand patches turned cream color. On our port hand a sharp volcanic peak jutted out of the water for over twelve hundred feet, covered with lush green trees, with a white sandy beach and palm trees at the water's edge. As I conned us through the coral heads toward the town, I felt that this was what I had been born to do and had lived my life preparing for. There was nothing in the world I'd rather be doing.

As we neared the land and came in the lee of the island, it was no longer a struggle to hang on aloft as it had been earlier. Suddenly a brown coral head appeared close in front of us. I yelled for a hard turn to port—and the brown patch disappeared. It was a huge manta ray, eighteen or twenty feet across the wings. Little waves had been breaking on his back, and at first glance he looked exactly like coral a few inches below the surface.

Manta ray (PHOTO BY HOWARD CLEAVES)

We came to anchor off the town pier at the village of Rikitea, an idyllic Polynesian village, warm, sunny, and peaceful. The chief of port and police, M. Duquesne, a Frenchman, and his Polynesian second-in-command came out to welcome us, and in typical bureaucratic manner told us that what we wanted to do, i.e., stay here for a few days, was completely impossible. Having had an idea what local officialdom might be like, I had gotten letters from the French consul in Boston and the governor in Tahiti, giving us permission to visit Mangareva before officially entering French Polynesia at Tahiti, which is the normally required procedure. We had been warned to do this by a Scot, Peter Hamilton, who had had similar troubles at Mangareva.

Apparently, though, our letters would do no good. A new governor had been appointed at Tahiti and was apparently jealous of his new authority, so we were told we had to go. Fortunately, Sally speaks pretty good French. Ashore, at Chief Duquesne's office and house, she explained that we needed fresh water, as well as to have our wash done. More important, it would be a real tragedy for us not to be able to visit his beautiful island after having sailed so far. It would be impossible to sail an extra two thousand miles—one thousand miles to Tahiti and then back again upwind. If we followed the rules, we would simply have to miss visiting his island altogether. Finally, the chief agreed to radio the governor in Tahiti for permission for us to stay, pointing out that this was a Saturday, so there would be some delay in getting an answer. Meanwhile Sally, Danny, and I could go ashore, but not Mouse and Sandy, who had no visas (not needed, the consul had assured us). More protestations on Sally's part—the boys would be so disappointed not to see such a wonderful island, and especially the *wahines*. Surely a Frenchman would understand! Finally he relented and said OK, but not to go up in the mountains—"*La bombe, vous connaissez!*" Well, we didn't know, but got the idea, and also the clear impression that he was doing his very best for us. It sure helps to speak French, and it's even better if you have a female intermediary.

Ashore, the island was as attractive as it had appeared from *Loon*. A wide sand footpath extended from an enormous church at one end of the village to open country at the other end. There were no cars or motorbikes. Everything was relaxed, quiet, peaceful, and perfectly lovely. The path was lined with stones on the edges, had coconut and breadfruit trees overhead, and tiny houses with clean yards set back from it. Their windows were unglazed, but had curtains made of bright *pareu* cloth, which has taken the place of *tapa*, once made from the bark of palm trees. There were the usual black Polynesian pigs tethered by their hind legs to trees in the yards. Chickens and friendly dogs wandered about. Most yards had at least one banana tree as well.

We were the center of curious groups of friendly and very appealing children, some of mixed Chinese and Polynesian ancestry (Chinamen are the storekeepers throughout Polynesia). Some were sailing model outrigger canoes with pareu sails in the harbor. Older men wore flowers behind one ear or the other, in the native fashion, indicating whether they were attached to a girl or free for adventure. Finally we came to a store, run by an elderly Frenchman with elephantiasis—a mightily swollen leg and ankle—who sold ice-cold Hinano beer from Tahiti. Finding cold beer in this already delightful and friendly place seemed the ultimate in luxury.

Back on board after a delightful walk beyond the village ashore, we entertained Chief Duquesne and his lieutenant, who was half-Polynesian, for cocktails. In spite or our stumbling French, we all had a fine time, and it was becoming more and more apparent that the duration of our stay was somewhat open to persuasion.

Sunday was a lazy day. After washing up *Loon* and airing our blankets up the masts on halyards, we took our washing ashore to a Mangarevan lady who had agreed to do it for us. We thus established a hostage ashore—she wasn't going to start on it on Sunday, and we couldn't leave until we got it back!

A very handsome and friendly native, Francois, then came out in his outrigger canoe with presents for us—two stalks of bananas, a lovely conch shell, and an offer of the use of his *pirogue,* which we gladly accepted. The next day he and the lieutenant came by in the official launch, towing a larger, very narrow outrigger canoe (to be used as a tender for going ashore later), and asked us to come for a day of fishing and diving on the reef. Of course we accepted, and were soon motoring out in the launch to an idyllic small island, or *motu,* with a smooth sandy beach partly shaded by coconut palms. A Mangarevan family was living on it temporarily, to take advantage of the excellent fishing. The mother and father were off for the day, leaving a girl of six or seven in charge of her much younger brother. Polynesian children, wherever we saw them, seemed mature, responsible, and happy, like these two. We never saw temper tantrums or adolescent problems. In days gone by, children were often given by their parents to other adult friends to bring up. Polynesian children are still loved, but not spoiled, by the whole adult community.

Danny and the boys joined Francois for spearfishing on the outer reef, while Sally and I snorkeled and swam out to join them. On the way we were not pleased to meet a shark, six to seven feet long, who swam up and peered in my faceplate. Since we were a couple of hundred yards from shore, I could only peer back and hope we looked unappetizing. I guess we must have, since he went on his way without trying to eat us. It's quite surprising how really ugly a shark looks when faced up close. He didn't seem streamlined or particularly well adapted to his medium, just rather fat in the middle, with a very unattractive face. I was glad to see him go.

We swam on out to the reef, but the fishermen had gone ahead, so, after some superb diving on the reef, Sally and I started back to the motu. This trip we walked on top of the coral as far as we could, in less than knee-deep water, in hopes of avoiding the shark. No such luck. On the long clumsy walk in our swim fins, we were escorted, in fact herded, by two sharks. At first I could scare them away a few feet by smacking the water near them with my fish spear, but they soon got so aggressive that I was actually hitting them with it to keep them off. Finally, after what seemed a very long and unpleasant walk, we made it back to shore with all parts still intact. Later on, Francois and the boys came back laden with fish. When we told them about our sharks, Francois said that they always followed people hoping to get some fish, and that there was nothing to worry about. It would have saved us some anguish if we'd known that, but I, for one, would have been good and scared anyway. On the way back to Rikitea, where the fish were divided up among the villagers, Francois casually skinned and ate one of his catch raw. He seemed delighted with it, and just as unconcerned as we would be opening a can of sardines.

Mangareva, in spite of how happy it seemed to us, has had its tragic past. A French missionary had arrived when the island supported something like forty thousand inhabitants, but after many years of his rule, the population was decimated to only a tenth of its original number. In his fervor to teach Christianity and stamp out sin, he had also stamped out the joy of life for the Polynesians. He put all girls in an enormous nunnery, outlawed dancing and feasts and made the men build the gigantic church at the end of the village. The church can seat far more than the whole current population. He also made them build some kind of a Christian church or chapel wherever a native religious artifact had been. When he was finally relieved by the French governor in his old age, and it was pointed out to him that most of the natives had died off in his reign, he answered, "Never mind. Their souls are all in heaven!" Since his time, the French administration has been more enlightened, and the inhabitants seem healthy and happy. This improvement has also apparently been happening in the Marquesas, where in previous times, including when we were there in the *Mary*, the population had fallen to very low levels. Disease, brought by white men, was rampant then and left mostly untreated by the missionaries. Things are better now, and populations are growing again. Native art is returning, as is the joy of life.

Our Polaroid camera came in as handy here as it had in the Galápagos. The lieutenant was very pleased to have pictures taken of himself and his son, to send to his parents in Tahiti. Melanie, who did our wash, and even Chief Duquesne, were very pleased to have pictures of themselves. A Polaroid camera is a wonderful tool for establishing friendly relations, and it let us give people something they really prized.

By this time a radio message had arrived, saying we must go to Tahiti immediately with no stops on the way. Fortunately, our wash wasn't done, *Loon* hadn't been watered, and Chief Duquesne hadn't put the finishing touches on a poem he wanted to write in *Loon*'s log. All these problems got us another day before we had to leave for the thousand-mile run to the west.

Our friendly send-off included repeated directives to go straight, with no stops on the way, but when we were about five miles from Rikitea, out of sight of the town because of an intervening hill, the coral six fathoms under us looked so beautiful that we couldn't resist anchoring for a morning of scuba diving. By lunchtime our air tanks were empty, and we saw a French destroyer approaching. Much to our consternation, our anchor was fouled on a coral head, and we couldn't go down to free it until the tanks were pumped up again, which would take over an hour. Then the chief's launch appeared, and I thought we really were in trouble. Much to our relief, it was the lieutenant, who simply asked if the diving was good and free of sharks. He said the destroyer had reported us to the chief, and that he thought we had been a new vessel coming in. He wished us an enthusiastic "bon voyage" and headed home. We freed the hook and went on our way.

Our first day at sea on this leg of our voyage started out as the perfect lazy sail, with light fair winds as we drifted along beneath the spinnaker on a smooth Pacific ocean—just what "yachting" is popularly believed to be like, and the first sail like this we had had in many a month. We celebrated with a supper of roast chicken (whole from a can), gravy, peas and onions, rice, and gingerbread with chocolate sauce for desert. Not bad for almost four thousand miles from our last supply port.

Two days later we made a landfall on a Tuomotu atoll called Mururoa, which according to our *Pacific Pilot* had a good pass and was uninhabited. This seemed like an ideal island to stop at, and we couldn't see any way that the authorities would ever hear about it. As we closed the island, we noticed what seemed to be a couple of masts on the beach, then saw that they were not only tipped but seemed to be varying their angle. We wondered if this could be a new wreck rolling in the surf, but as we got closer we saw that they were crane booms swinging draglines into the surf to get coral for a road being built on the beach. Then we saw the pass, and inside it a floating dry dock and navy vessels anchored in the lagoon. It dawned on us, a little late, that this must be the French atom-bomb island. We sailed on, trying our very best to look as un-spylike and unaware of what was going on as possible. Now we knew about "*La bombe, vous connaissez!*"

The rest of our sail to Tahiti was in rather fluky winds, often ahead, and with increasing frequency and strength as we progressed westward. First came short, steep seas that were hard to beat up against, then a gusty west wind. We shortened down for the gusts, but then didn't have enough drive to push *Loon* into the seas in the comparatively calm periods. Finally, deeply frustrated, we pushed ahead under jib and mizzen with the engine slowly turning over—a terrible fix for dedicated sailors to find themselves in! Ocean passages, even in the aptly named Pacific, are not always a bed of roses. We had the feeling that we were never going to break out of that low. The wind came up even harder, with increasing seas, slowing us to almost a standstill. Finally I had the idea that if we headed north, we might be able to sail away from the approaching low. In the southern hemisphere, the winds blow clockwise into a low, and by sailing north in a northwest wind, we hoped we were escaping the low. This seemed to work, and the weather got better as we sailed north.

A few mornings out, I had an urge to look into the bilge, and when I did, found it was filled with water up to the engine mounting bolts. Since *Loon* is welded aluminum, the most probable way she could be leaking was through the shaft packing gland, so I tightened this up and pumped her out. The next morning the bilge was filled up again, which gave us all quite a jolt. Sally quietly ran up her DR position and found there was an atoll not too far away, but without a pass, making landing possible but only in a very dire emergency. Meanwhile, I did some more looking and found the trouble, much to our relief. When *Loon* was built, a copper nail had been inadvertently driven through a bulkhead into the copper tubing leading from a seacock to the salt-water pump in the galley. This had corroded enough so that a tiny stream of water was shooting into the bilge in the same area as the packing nut on the shaft. Once found, it was an easy matter to bend the pipe out from the bulkhead and wrap it with plastic electrical tape. End of leak.

Seven days out from Mangareva, we sighted the perfectly symmetrical cone of the tiny island of Mehitia, sixty miles east of Tahiti. Not too long after passing abeam of it, we caught sight of Tahiti itself. That evening we began a fabulous sail along the north shore of that majestic island. As night fell, the island was brightly lit by the moon. Soon we saw the lights (Coleman lanterns) of fishermen looking for crayfish on the reef. The fair breeze died, and a gentle offshore zephyr carried us the scent of burning coconut husks. The smell brought me suddenly and very pleasantly back to the Polynesia of 1929.

What a delightful sail that was, with a gentle breeze over smooth water and a whiff of boyhood coming from a beautiful island in the moonlight. It was everything I could have hoped for. The moon was so bright, and the range lights leading into Papeete harbor so clear, that we decided to go on instead of waiting for daylight. We anchored at one-thirty in the morning, and all sat on deck for a long time, looking at this most romantic island and listening to the roosters, which crow all night in Polynesia.

None of us was sleepy, and we speculated about how the Polynesians themselves had gotten here originally and where they had come from. Their legends indicate that they migrated from somewhere in the west, but are not definite about the route or starting point. Because ruling-class Polynesians have Caucasian features, some archaeologists believed that they were descended from an Aryan people in India. The nonruling class is more Negroid, and it has been suggested that this characteristic came from Micronesian and Melanesian stock picked up in the course of migration from the west.

Thor Heyerdahl has said that easterly trade winds and west-flowing currents make this route improbable and has suggested that drift voyages from South America brought settlers to the islands. To back his hypothesis, he sailed an Egyptian-type reed boat from the Mediterranean to South America, and a balsa raft from Ecuador to Polynesia. In support of his theory, he cites Polynesian legends of red-bearded white visitors to the islands, and the presence in the islands of such native American plants as the sweet potato. More recently he has suggested that drift voyages from Asia to the islands of the British Columbian coast, and from there to the South Pacific, also brought settlers to Polynesia, perhaps before the appearance of Caucasians from South America. He describes the striking similarities between the body types and culture of North American Indians living on these islands and the Polynesians themselves.

Professor Barry Fell of Harvard, a linguist and expert in early forms of writing, believes that the Caucasian stock in Polynesia came from Libya, not Asia. Libyans were descended from Greeks and Anatolians, as well as Berbers, and apparently served as officers in early Egyptian ships. Fell finds many Greek roots in Polynesian languages and points out the similarities between Greek and Polynesian myths, as well as the identical designs of Libyan and Polynesian tattooing. On my first trip to the South Pacific I heard a story in the Tuomotus almost identical to the Greek myth of Orpheus and Eurydice, as well as the legend of the great flood.

To archaeologists without any seagoing experience in small boats, an ocean seemed much more of a barrier to travel by ancient people than it actually was. It was generally accepted until recently that it was impossible before Columbus's time to cross the Atlantic, and that Polynesia must have been settled over a long period of time by short voyages between relatively nearby islands. Even Heyerdahl assumed that Polynesia must have been settled by boats or rafts that couldn't sail upwind effectively, and hence were reached mainly by drift voyages such as his *Ra* and *Kon Tiki* expeditions. Now we know that Polynesians were very competent seamen and navigators, and made long voyages between Hawaii and New Zealand. The more we learn about so-called "primitive" people, the more we find that many of them were undertaking long voyages as routine trading operations. This means that they could not have relied entirely on downwind drift operations.

Fell, on the basis of translations of Celtic, Basque, Phoenician, Libyan, and other inscriptions, has presented evidence that these people all colonized the east coast of America as long as 2,500 years ago, leaving observatories for determining the time of the winter solstice, and other megalithic monuments, proving their presence long before Columbus's time. They even extended their exploration and colonization up the Mississippi River and into its western tributaries.

It is generally recognized that Norsemen colonized Greenland and Newfoundland in the period from A.D. 800 to A.D. 1400, but Fell has deciphered extensive rock inscriptions near Toronto in Canada showing that a Nordic king, Woden-lithi, spent five months in that area in roughly 1700 B.C. on a trading voyage to exchange European cloth with the Indians, who supplied him with copper ingots to take back to Europe. Apparently, this was a well-established trade route, and depended on the warmer climate of that time, which made it possible to sail the westward voyage in the high-latitude easterlies and return on the normal west-wind route still used by sailors today. Presumably with the return of a colder climate, this route was abandoned.

It now seems very clear that those we used to think of as primitive people had a marine technology that let them undertake routine voyages across both the Atlantic and Pacific. After all, it's not so very hard to sail across an ocean. Nowadays people are doing it in smaller and less suitable boats each year. Several people have even rowed across the Atlantic, and a husband and wife are currently attempting the Pacific by oar. I guess the conclusion has to be that the settlers of Polynesia came from many different places at various times and were absorbed into the population, just as they still are. It was nice to feel that we were part of an ancient tradition.

In the morning, after only two or three hours of sleep, Tahiti wasn't quite as glamorous. There were cars and light motorbikes everywhere, and all the bustle of a busy metropolis. A pilot came out to tell us where to tie up and stood silently on deck as we dropped a bow anchor, then backed her close to the shore, and put stern lines out to bollards on a muddy bank. Next to us was a double-ended Colin Archer-type ketch, *Tangaroa,* with a handsome, pleasant, and helpful couple from Seattle and their two children. Then began the usual rounds ashore to customs and the port captain, where we had to leave our guns for our stay in French Polynesia. After that, we went on to the office of our cordial agent, Preston Moore, where we found an enormous pile of very welcome mail waiting for us. Dinner ashore, then Dan and the boys went out for a night on the town.

The next morning Mouse's parents, Jane and Walter Page, arrived from New York to cruise with us. The lovely steaks they had brought with them were immediately confiscated by customs officers, on the weak excuse that they might bring in animal diseases. I'll bet the officers had a good steak dinner that night. We spent several busy days cleaning up *Loon,* shopping to resupply her and trying to find out how we could ship her home at the end of our stay. Then we saw the two boys off on the plane for home. They had had only a couple of hectic days in Tahiti—not their ideal, but college was waiting.

Now we were ready to start our cruise in the romantically named Isles Sou le Vent—the leeward islands near Tahiti. After another round with customs, port captain, the Physosanitaire (Plant Health Department), and immigration, we were finally given permission to sail to Moorea—fifteen miles away. Each time we made this passage, we had to go through the same red tape, which if you didn't speak French could easily take a whole day. With practice and minimal French, I gradually learned how to do it all in an hour, but on one occasion I forgot to give a crew list to one of the bureaucrats. We were met on the beach at Moorea by a jeep carrying four soldiers armed with rifles, who demanded to see the captain. When it turned out that I understood French and was cooperative, it was all adjusted with the crew list in triplicate and smiles on all sides.

Moorea has frequently been called the most beautiful island in the world, with good reason. Like Tahiti, it's volcanic, but much steeper and more dramatic than the bigger island. Several volcanic cones have eroded away, leaving the sharp spikes of lava plugs behind. A barrier reef surrounds the island, with passes into the two large bays on the west side, Pao Pao and Papetoi. Coconut palms grow on the white-sand beaches, and right behind them are open valleys between steep-sided green mountains coming down almost to the shore. When we were there, Moorea was much more rural than Papeete, with very few cars and a much more relaxed and typically Polynesian atmosphere. We anchored in Papetoi Bay, certainly one of the loveliest harbors I've ever been in, then took a walk ashore, up a little-used dirt road into the valley at the head of the harbor.

That afternoon a very colorful 35-foot ketch called *Diogene* came in. She had a well-cocked-up bowsprit, a racy sheer, and red sails with a big yellow Maltese cross on the mainsail. A man, his wife, and four children were living on board. He had been an automobile salesman in France and had traded his car for the hull of *Diogene* in Costa Rica, where he and his boys finished building the boat. They had then set off to sail around the world. His wife apparently had no real interest in sailing, but gallantly came along anyway, and had managed to make a very homelike atmosphere in the tiny cabin of *Diogene*. They had even brought along a small, French-speaking green parrot (how sophisticated can a parrot get?) and a very aquatic fox terrier. The family had spent the winter in Tahiti so the boys could go to school. It was an eye-opener to me that a family who obviously had very little money, but a lot of determination, could successfully sail around the world, supporting themselves with odd jobs wherever they could find them. It helped that the oldest boy was an expert welder, but they all pitched in and did their share. They planned to go on to Noumea the next winter, so that the boys could go to a French school again.

We have often met people in our sailing travels who say how much they wish they could do what we were doing, but don't have enough money, can't give up their jobs, their children have to go to school, their wives don't like sailing, and so on. The crew of *Diogene* did it in spite of all these difficulties. It can be done if you *want* to enough, and we've met people over and over again who are having the adventure of a lifetime sailing to exotic places in spite of all kinds of difficulties.

Ashore in Papetoi Bay, under some magnificent trees, including an enormous banyan tree, and surrounded by exotic tropical flowers, nestled the small, green, wooden house of the Kellums, whom we soon met. They had come to Moorea in the early 1920s, on a big schooner belonging to Med Kellum's father, had fallen in love with the island and each other, married, and settled there. They later owned about half of the island and farmed it for many years, but recently sold most of their land to the French government for an agricultural research station. They are a most charming couple, and when they came out and invited us to go on a picnic, we were delighted. They suggested we leave *Loon,* and go with them in their small sloop.

As we left, Med Kellum asked me if I had put out enough scope, to which I replied, "Sure." Other boats were anchored close to shore with a stern line to a coconut tree, but we had anchored out in the middle, preferring the privacy this gave us. After a great day of skin diving and a picnic on the beach, we sailed back to Papetoi Bay. Med quietly remarked that he couldn't see *Loon.* I couldn't believe it, and insisted that a coconut tree on the beach was her mast, and that she was just where we had left her. As we got nearer, we found that Med was absolutely right. *Loon* just wasn't there anymore. We were appalled and speechless. After a frantic search, we found her anchored and hidden behind a point on the other side of the harbor. A native had noticed her drifting out to sea, and had towed her into this cove with an outboard on his outrigger canoe, where he re-anchored her. Apparently a *williwaw,* or very severe squall, had blown down the valley, and she had dragged into deep water. She was on her way out the pass when he rescued her. Fortunately this all happened on a Saturday, or he wouldn't have been there.

This taught me not to be too sure that the ways of doing things that I had learned at home were better than those I met abroad. There are often good reasons for doing things differently, because local conditions often evolve their own best solutions. After this, we made *Loon*'s stern fast to a tree whenever we could. It's pretty hard to drag a coconut tree with a 45-foot yawl, and besides, tying up near other boats is an easy way to meet a lot of interesting people. With Med Kellum's help as an interpreter, we were able to thank our rescuer in an appropriate manner. Med needled me about this episode periodically during our stay, and I deserved it.

Now began a month of more relaxed and unhurried cruising. We had time to make friends ashore and on other boats. Our particular boat friends were the Hansons on *Tangaroa*. They were a very appealing couple with a young boy and a teenage daughter. The children were keeping up their studies with the Calvert School lessons. It was a great experience for the boy, but Polynesian cruising was not so ideal for a teenage girl isolated on a boat and with no friends of her own age to enjoy. Paula and Earl Shenk on an Alden steel ketch called *Eleuthera* also became very good friends. They had sailed by themselves from Seattle, with stops in the Marquesas and Tuomotus, and were spending the winter in the islands near Tahiti.

We got to know some of the local people through the Kellums. Once they took us to a feast celebrating the marriage of one of their friends, who was part French and part Polynesian. It was quite a party. Everyone had an easy, friendly, and innocently risqué sense of fun, and an uncomplicated joy in living that is hard to find in more sophisticated parts of the world.

From Moorea, with the Pages and Dan on board, we had an overnight sail to Raiatea, a less developed island. Market day happened once a week, when *goelets* (strictly meaning schooners, but actually any small inter-island transports) filled with guitar-playing men and seasick women came for the festivities. Polynesian females feel obliged to be seasick. We even had them suffering on board *Loon,* tied up to the quay in harbor. A few people came in sailing outrigger canoes, others in the goelets or on buses. The food for sale included sea turtles and pigs, as well as breadfruit, mangoes, taro, watermelons, and many vegetables. We visited a lovely waterfall there and had a fresh water swim and bath.

On Tahaa, a separate island enclosed by the same barrier reef as Raiatea, we were visited one evening by two natives with their guitars. We asked them on board, and spent a fun evening listening to their songs and watching them dance on our much too small deck to drums consisting of spoons that we clacked together or beat on the bottom of a cooking pot. It doesn't take much equipment to make a party go in Polynesia, and soon we were dancing along with them.

On Bora Bora we met a very small Tahitian ketch—a double-ended Colin Archer-type of about twenty-five feet called *Atom*. She was sailed singlehandedly by a Frenchman, M. Jean Gau, who, when he wasn't sailing, was a pastry chef in New York. He worked on a four-on, four-off schedule: that is, he worked four years as a chef, then took four years off to sail around the world. This was his second trip, and he had a good many Atlantic crossings to his credit. It was Jean Gau and *Atom* who had taken fifty-five days to reach the Galápagos from Panama. He told us that he then planned to visit Pitcairn, and took seventy-five more days to get there. It was too rough for him to anchor, but when the Pitcairners suggested he wait a day or two for better weather so that he could visit the island, he told them he didn't have time to wait, and sailed on to Tahiti, another thirty-day passage!

Nearing the completion of his first circumnavigation, he was off the New Jersey beach approaching New York when an airplane flew overhead and dropped a package with a red ribbon attached. Jean said he knew exactly what it meant even before he opened it, and he was right. It contained a message saying he was in the path of a hurricane. His story continued, "I said to myself, 'Jean, after zis long way around ze world, now you are in ze path of ze 'urricane, and you've 'ad it.' " "But," he continued, "I go below and pour myself a Pernod, and I feel better. Ze 'urricane blow for two days. *Atom* she heel over to sixty degrees, but on ze serd day my hinclinometer say only fifty-eight degrees. I say to myself, 'Jean, ze 'urricane is blowing itself out. You 'aven't 'ad it after all.' I pour myself a Pernod and I feel *much* better!"

A whole hurricane told in two Pernods! Many years later, *Atom* was wrecked on the beach near Ocean City, Maryland, but a collection was taken up, a bulldozer hired to dig a ditch to deep water, and *Atom* was refloated. Sad to say, Jean has since died. He was an extraordinary person, and, in spite of not having had time to wait a day or two at Pitcairn, he gave every evidence of enjoying people and life ashore.

I did a stupid thing at Bora Bora. Before leaving for the Tuomotus, we had a long, beer-filled lunch at the local hotel, and as I was conning *Loon* out of the harbor from the spreaders, Danny told me that the engine was overheating. I remembered I had been washing the bilge that morning and had forgotten to reconnect the cooling water to the engine. We set sail, and I waited for the engine temperature to fall well below boiling on the gauge before I gingerly loosened the cap to the water reservoir with my foot. No steam came out, so, thinking I was safe, I reached down and took off the cap with my hand—and a jet of boiling water spurted out and hit me in the face and chest. Fortunately, I had dark glasses on, so it didn't get in my eyes. We decided not to go to sea that night. I had one morphine tablet, a couple of scotches, and went to bed.

We set off the next morning for Rangiroa. I figured if I got really sick, we could always alter course for Tahiti, and to play it safe I injected myself with antibiotics for several days to prevent infection. I looked an awful mess, blistered, swollen, and wrapped up in Vaseline gauze and pressure bandages, but happily suffered no permanent ill effects. The crew very thoughtfully let me sleep in the first two nights of our four-day passage to Rangiroa.

We found the pass in the reef without too much trouble and motored in against a strong head current. Most atoll passes, which are on the leeward side, have a current running out, since the seas from the constant trade winds break over the windward side of the reef and have to flow out somewhere. Rangiroa is a big atoll, and once through the pass we were on the leeward side of the lagoon in quite a chop. We tried anchoring in a couple of places, but it was hard to find one free enough of coral heads to make it safe. Just as we were wondering what to do, the chief's daughter came out and offered to pilot us to a protected anchorage in the pass itself, which she did. We put down bow and stern anchors, checked them with aqualungs, and were quite happy and snug.

Ashore, several boats, including outrigger canoes, an outboard or two, and a small sailboat, were pulled up on the beach, which was shaded by coconut palms. A few simple houses and a small wooden church completed the village. Like Mangareva, there were dogs and pigs, but the village was not nearly as neat and gave an impression of poverty compared to the high islands. Life is obviously much harder on the atolls, where there is limited fresh water and gardens don't grow as well in the poor soil. Even the light is sharp and hard—brilliant white sand contrasting with deep shadow. Perhaps this is the reason that the Tuomotuans don't share the lackadaisical attitude so prevalent on the high islands. The sandy land only reaches a few feet above high tide and, during hurricanes, is often completely covered by surf. The natives climb coconut trees, cut off the fronds, and lash themselves aloft until the water goes down. Their only income comes from *copra*—dried coconut meat—and from pearl shell, and a very occasional pearl. We were told that diving for pearl shell was no longer done here because the sharks were too aggressive. Fortunately, Danny didn't hear about this until after he had speared some very fine fish.

Rangiroa presented me with the solution to the problem that had been bothering me ever since the Galápagos, that is, what to pump nutrient-rich deep water into, in an experiment aimed at artificially reproducing the high productivity and stable ecosystem of natural upwelling areas, such as the Peru current. There are a great many atolls stretching across the Pacific and Indian oceans, most of which have fairly complete coral rings around them, with relatively shallow water in the lagoons. They would provide ideal ready-made containers, since they are built on the top of steep-sided volcanic cones. They are also in the trade wind belt, and have, because of this, a wind-driven stirring system, with a surface downwind flow and a deep upwind return. The shallow bottom and coral ring would contain the cold water and keep it from sinking down again, as well as providing a container for whatever was to be grown inside—sort of a coral corral. It's obvious there's enough energy in the trade winds to bring deep water to the surface, since that's what causes natural upwelling. The Tuomotus and many other atolls are situated in the Trades, and nutrient-rich water, which is only 1,500 feet or so below the surface, could easily be pumped into a lagoon with pumps driven by windmills.

We know from past experiments that the productivity of ocean water, which is very low in the open tropical oceans, can be enormously increased by fertilization, either with sewage, commercial fertilizer, or natural upwelling. The reason for the low productivity of the open ocean is that phytoplankton organisms have silica or calcium shells, making them heavy, and when they die, they sink, taking the nutrients that they have concentrated from the surface water with them and adding to the supply in deep water, which is nutrient-rich worldwide.

There are a lot of fascinating experiments that could be done with deep water pumped into an atoll, but to me the most interesting would be to pump it in and leave it alone. It might be possible to reproduce the naturally occurring, efficient, highly productive, and, most important, stable food chain seen in natural upwelling areas. If so, this would be an enormous step forward, since productive agriculture on land is dependent on very large energy inputs in the form of tractor fuel and oil-dependent fertilizers, pesticides, and herbicides. This is expensive, hard on the land, and the chemicals are usually toxic and often carcinogenic. In addition, we are losing farmland at a very rapid rate, and much of the world seems to have run out of its food supply already. Protein deficiency is widespread in the world, and artificial upwelling into atolls might well be a cheap and efficient way of relieving it.

In addition to an experiment leaving things alone in the pumped-up water, one could select animals to harvest the phytoplankton that would grow in it. Anchovies, because of their position low on the food chain, would be one obvious choice. Baleen whales, which feed on zooplankton, which in turn feed on phytoplankton, would be another. This isn't as crazy as it sounds. People have captured whales unharmed by letting them swim through a noose and tightening it over the "small" just ahead of their flukes. They were transported to aquaria in nets passed around them and supported at the surface by floats. The nets were towed, and the whales swam along inside. We know that pregnant, plankton-eating whales swim up from Antarctica to calve in the tropical waters of the Pacific, so the towed journey wouldn't have to be a very long one.

A number of pregnant whales could be tagged with radio transmitters in Antarctica (as has been done with birds and turtles) so that their positions would be known, and then could be captured and towed into a nearby atoll. If whales could be grown in captivity, it would protect them from extermination, which the whaling industry, particularly of Russia and Japan, is in great danger of causing. Growth in captivity is, after all, what kept the American bison from being exterminated.

When I got home, I wrote this idea up in a couple of scientific journals.* Some time after the first paper was published, a group from Columbia's Lamont-Doherty Geological Observatory picked up the idea. They put a pipe down into deep water off St. Croix in the Virgin Islands and pumped it into small ponds on shore, where plankton growth was stimulated about 27-fold, in remarkably good agreement with the roughly 30-fold increase in the Peru current. They also observed rapid growth in a number of marine herbivores fed on the plankton, so the idea does work. I tried for a number of years to find financing for an actual experiment in an atoll, but never succeeded. Lots of people were interested, and I got letters from all over the world from people who would have liked to join the project, but no cash ever materialized, so unfortunately the experiment has never been done.

Pinchot, Gifford B. "Whale Culture—A Proposal." *Perspectives in Biology and Medicine* 10 (1966): 133.
———."Marine Farming." *Scientific American* 233 (1970): 15.

13

Much too soon, it was time to sail back to Tahiti so that the crew could catch their flights home. The downwind trip was warm and fast, and we spotted the peaks of Tahiti from sixty-five miles away. After reluctantly seeing the Pages, and later Danny, off to New York, Sally and I settled into a strange routine of relaxing in this tropical paradise and then struggling with the frustrating and complex arrangements for getting *Loon* shipped to Guadeloupe on her way home. This included getting plans for a cradle from Sparkman & Stephens, and then persuading a local boatyard to build it for us.

At the boatyard, we met three young engineers who were repairing a lovely Laurent Giles 35-foot sloop called *Easterling*, putting in new ribs and planks on both sides. They told us about being attacked one evening by a whale and stove in, first on one side and then on the other, halfway between the Galápagos and the Marquesas, 1,500 miles from shore. Water rushed in so fast, they said it sounded like a waterfall. They managed to slow the flow enough by stuffing rags and pillows in the holes, so that they could keep up with the rest by bailing with a bucket. (The overworked bilge pump had broken early in the adventure.) Realizing they were in for a long siege, they set up a schedule with one man bailing, one steering, and one sleeping. The next morning they were able to cover one of the leaks with a stainless-steel sheet, with nail holes punched around its edges, that they had brought along for just such an accident. They backed it up with towels and bedding compound next to the planking to make it as tight as possible. The leak on the other side was covered with a canvas patch held down by wooden strips around the edge. This worked much better than the metal sheet, since it conformed to the compound curve of the hull. The patches were put on the outside of the hull with the help of snorkels and masks. They were so good that *Easterling* was able to sail the 1,500 miles to the Marquesas, stay there two weeks, visit the Tuomotus, and finally end up in Tahiti for solid repairs.

Two of the three *Easterling* crew, Al Forsythe and Dick Anderson, had decided to return home, while the third, Bruce Katter, elected to sail the boat on around the world alone. The two who were leaving were just what we needed, and we offered them transportation from Nassau to their homes if they would look after *Loon* on the steamer from Tahiti to the Caribbean, and then sail with us from Guadeloupe to Nassau. This idea appealed to them, so, with all the details finally straightened out, Sally and I went back for a few peaceful and idyllic days at Moorea. Anchored in that superb harbor, it seemed absolute madness to go to all that trouble and fuss, just to get home for a cold winter of work in a laboratory. It was so tempting to find a way to stay on *Loon* in Polynesia. But my leave of absence was nearly over, and our New England consciences prevailed. We did go home, and when we got there the decision didn't seem any saner than it had when we were in Moorea.

We returned to Tahiti to load *Loon* aboard the steamer *Tahitien* for her trip home. We took her mizzen out by hand, with the help of friends, but left the mainmast in place. I had persuaded the mate of the *Tahitien* that this was OK, and that he could lift her with the ship's crane attached to a sling we had made up, which led to lifting rings welded to her keel. Normally, both masts would be taken out for shipping, but with the sling's hoisting point well aft of the mainmast, we were able to leave it in place, which greatly simplified the whole procedure, including her rerigging later on.

We hoisted her up on deck and lowered her into the cradle, only to find that it didn't quite fit, and that the steel rods that were supposed to hold down two timbers across her deck and keep her snug in the cradle were missing. With only two hours to go before sailing time, I hastily altered the cradle to fit, with the help of a couple of Tahitian carpenters. The mate supplied some wire rope and turnbuckles and even welded four rings on the deck of the steamer to lead them to. With this rig, she was held firmly to the deck as well as in the cradle.

We finished securing *Loon* just as the steamer's whistle announced her departure. I hurried down the gangplank with a milling crowd of giggling Tahitian girls, who had been saying their last fond farewells to their sailor friends and were probably already looking forward to their replacements. The shipyard owner was particularly glad to see me, since he had been afraid I was going to leave on the steamer without paying his bill.

The airplane was almost empty when Sally and I flew home, and one of the stewardesses, impressed by our suntans, I guess, asked how long we had been in Tahiti and whether we liked it there. We said we certainly did, but she was puzzled. She had flown in the day before and had visited Quinn's Bar (where all the sailors hang out) and the then-plush Hotel Tahiti. She felt that she had "done" Tahiti, wasn't very impressed, and wondered what we found so good about it. How can you explain that Polynesia has more to recommend it than a tough bar and a good hotel?

It takes a while to get into the relaxed, noncompetitive frame of mind that Polynesia encourages. You don't "do" Polynesia, you cast off some of your preoccupation with money and success and begin to understand and become part of that wonderfully beautiful place. I suppose this relaxed attitude has arisen because life, on the high islands at least, is comparatively easy. There isn't any winter to save up for, and not many bad times either. There have always been fish to catch and coconuts and fruit to eat, and it's never been necessary to work very hard to make a perfectly satisfactory living. Building a house is easy too—all you need are a few uprights and a roof of plaited coconut fronds. Windows and heating aren't needed.

We'd been in Polynesia long enough to absorb a little of this attitude, and it was a real shock to get back to the cutthroat competition of research at home. It was obvious that everyone was running as hard as they could to keep up, and, with luck, get ahead of the competition. It just wasn't quite so obvious, after our time in Polynesia, that what they were running after was really worth getting, or worth missing so many of the really important things in life. Sailing to foreign places, and especially to Polynesia, inevitably produces changes in your philosophy of life that make it very hard to go back to the singleminded pursuit of "success" that we take for granted in this country. When we got home, I did try to fit into the old high-pressure pattern again. It wasn't easy, nor was it completely successful.

Late in November, in the first snowstorm of the winter, Sally and I flew to St. Croix. I carried a new sling, made of two legs of one-inch wire rope spliced into a heavy ring, with shackles on the other ends to fit the lifting rings welded to *Loon*'s keel. The whole thing weighed close to a hundred pounds. From St. Croix we took an island-hopping Convair to Guadeloupe. Having flown on Caribbean airlines before, I got out at every stop to make sure the sling wasn't left along the way and, sure enough, was able to prevent it from happening at one stop. By the time we were halfway to Guadeloupe, most of the other passengers had gotten off, and I made friends with the pilot, a jolly, rotund Puerto Rican, who let me sit on the flight deck but wouldn't go so far as to let me fly the airplane. The Convair had JATO (for "jet assisted takeoff") written in large letters on its side, and I asked the pilot about it. He said the plane really did have JATO, a good safety factor in some of the very short fields on his run. He showed me the arming switch overhead and the firing button on the stick. I asked if he had ever needed it, and he told me about a day flying out of St. Thomas with a full load and a hill at the end of the runway. When the tower told him that his number-two engine was on fire, he shut it down. When I asked how the JATO worked, he said with a happy grin, "Forgot to use it!" So much for that safety factor.

Early the next morning, after arriving at Guadeloupe, we went to the quay and found the *Tahitien* already docked, with *Loon* intact on deck. The hassle first began with customs. We were told that we would have to hire an agent for a fee of several hundred dollars to clear *Loon* through. I balked at this, and went to the Duane's office while the bosun was unloading a couple of powerboats. I was given a bunch of papers to fill out but told the officer I would send Sally up to do it, while I saw to *Loon*'s unloading. He asked with much suspicion if she could speak French. I said, "Sure, and much better than I do. That wouldn't be hard, would it?" This, in my bad French, so disarmed him that when Sally got there the papers were all filled out. All she had to do was sign them.

The unloading wasn't quite so easy. The bosun, who was in charge, was a character from Marseille. His only garments were a pair of the shortest shorts I had ever seen, a pair of sneakers, and a sheath knife, without sheath, sandwiched between him and the shorts. Why he didn't cut off either the shorts or his rear end, I have never been able to understand. He was extensively tattooed in green, and the French he spoke was, to me at least, as exotic as his appearance, so that it was very hard for us to communicate.

There was a problem with *Loon*'s unloading, because there wasn't a shackle big enough to go around the three-inch one on the block of the ship's crane, and the three-inch shackle wouldn't fit through the lifting ring in my sling. Apparently there had been an adequate shackle, but "boats" had thrown it overboard in a fit of pique. Finally, we got him to fasten our sling to the crane shackle with a number of turns of wire rope. This worked fine, and they lowered *Loon*, with Sally and me on deck, into the water, where she lay in the scorching sun next to the black side of the *Tahitien*. I rigged the spreaders and shrouds on the mizzenmast, and the fifty-ton ship's crane picked it up and gently lowered it into place. By this time I was about to pass out from heat and the worry of unloading her. We started the engine and motored around to the yacht harbor, where we put Dick and Al ashore so that they could say good-bye to friends on the *Tahitien*. No sooner had we anchored in the harbor than we were greeted with another problem. A native customs officer saw our American ensign and assumed that we had sailed in from a foreign port without entering through customs. He motioned me to come ashore, and when I got there, he gave me a solid half-hour tongue-lashing for entering without a quarantine flag, putting crew ashore without the consent of customs and immigration, and so on, *ad nauseam*. This was not easy to take at the end of that very full day, but there was nothing I could do but wait until he ran down and then explain that all the required formalities had already been taken care of. He received the explanation with a grunt, turned his back and stalked off.

The day did have a better ending, though. We all repaired to the local yacht club, where they served ice-cold local beer, unpasteurized and unfiltered, with a layer of yeast on the bottom. It was the most delicious beer I've ever tasted.

There was one more frustration before we left. It seemed a shame to leave the cradle in Guadeloupe, but when I asked for a quote on shipping it to the states, they wanted almost as much as it had cost to ship *Loon* from Tahiti—a good deal more than the cradle was worth. Lumber is scarce in the Caribbean, but when I tried to sell the very big and valuable pieces to a local lumberyard, I found no takers. The locals had me over a barrel, and they knew it. They were going to get the cradle free, so why pay for it? I was so mad I almost burned it on the dock, but probably would have been jailed for arson if I had.

Loon had come through in fine shape. Dick and Al had cleaned and repainted her bottom, and except for some tiny spots of white paint that had blown on her when the *Tahitien*'s crew painted their derrick on the voyage, she looked great. In spite of minor frustrations, we had fared very well, and set off for our trip home looking forward to good cruising in the steady trade winds and clear tropical waters of the Caribbean.

We weren't disappointed. Dick and Al proved to be a very skillful and congenial crew. They had lots of local knowledge in these waters and were able to show us the best of islands and cruising there. They were also very experienced skin divers, and their spears provided delicious fish and crayfish for *Loon*'s dinner menus. Conch they picked up on the sandy bottom and introduced us to the pleasure of eating these raw, or in hot conch chowder.

Our first island was St. Barts. Its small, completely protected harbor was edged with stone quays with enormous bollards, built for old sailing men-of-war to be careened and have their bottoms cleaned. It was a duty-free port, and we replenished our supplies with scotch for three dollars a bottle and Mount Gay rum for forty-eight cents. On Sunday morning we heard strains of a Bach cantata drifting over the harbor. One of the local churches was broadcasting it over a loudspeaker, and we realized how much we had missed that kind of music on our long cruise. After a couple of days of shopping, wandering around the island on foot, and cleaning the last of the grime off *Loon,* we set off for an overnight run to Virgin Gorda.

We entered at Spanish Town, then spent a wonderful morning at the Baths, a jumble of enormous, round granite boulders as big as small houses, right on the beach. It's a fascinating and eerie place to explore, swimming or walking through the narrow passages and bigger caves between the boulders, sometimes in deep shadow, or, where there are openings, in bright sunlight. The boulders are so smooth and round that they must have been ground together for a long time, yet how this could happen in the absence of glaciers is hard to understand. It's a mystery how they came to Virgin Gorda in the first place.

After a visit to Peter Island, we went on to St. Thomas in the American Virgins, where we were amazed at the number of buoys. There hadn't been any at all in the Galápagos and Polynesia. In spite of their profusion here, a freighter had run aground just beneath the lighthouse at the harbor entrance on Christmas Eve. Apparently, the skipper had started celebrating early, and was drunk when he arrived. Even the best of navaids aren't any help against that hazard.

We met Dick and Al's friend Ed Boden in Charlotte Amalie. Ed was sailing around the world alone in his Virtue Class sloop, *Kittiwake.* The last time we heard, he was still cruising. He is a man of many skills, and when he runs short of money, he stops for a while at a port along the way, gets to know the locals, and makes enough fixing outboards or surveying land to carry him on to his next stopping place.

Our next port, after a four-day passage, was Cockburn, on the lee side of San Salvador in the Bahamas. This is believed to be the island where Columbus made his landfall at the end of his first transatlantic voyage. Cockburn was a tiny village on a beach covered with beautiful shells. We anchored in crystal-clear water over a white-sand bottom and spent a couple of days exploring.

We then set sail in the late afternoon for the forty-mile run to Galliot Cut in the Exumas. This was a night of careful navigation, star sights, moon sights, and RDF bearings. Galliot Cut is a narrow passage between two of the Exuma islands, and the only navigational aid was a light that couldn't be seen on the approach from San Salvador. The Exumas are low and hard to identify, since they all look very much alike. Dick and Al had made this passage before, so we were glad to have them aboard.

We were relieved to find the cut and bucked a three-knot current going through. From there we went on to an anchorage behind Cave Cay, where we had some successful but nervous skin diving. Dick and Al speared some squirrel fish, but we were escorted the whole time by the biggest barracuda I'd ever seen. I reminded myself that things look about a third bigger than they actually are when you're underwater, but it didn't change the fact that he was as long as I was tall. He swam within a few feet of us, and kept opening and closing his mouth in a most unpleasant and suggestive way. He didn't bother us beyond that, but when he was joined by a very large shark, well over ten feet, I suggested to Sally that we get the hell out of there. Dick and Al, being braver, stayed in.

The next day we had a good, very fast, and, for me, tense sail to a tiny protected cove at Harvey Cay. It was nervous work because we were on the west side of the Exumas, where it's very shallow. In that clear water the bottom and the coral heads are all too obvious. The available charts were pretty useless, and we operated with the *Yachtsman's Guide to the Bahamas,* which has sketch charts and drawings of the harbors, but isn't very specific about soundings. Added to this, we had lots of wind and were tearing along at hull speed. It was too rough to judge the depth by color from aloft, so we hoped that the note on the sketch chart saying there were twelve to fourteen feet of water on the way to Harvey Cay was correct, and that there weren't any uncharted coral heads. If there were, we didn't find them. Once we were anchored, the boys managed to spear three big langoustes for a delicious supper.

The next day it was blowing even harder for our sail to Allen Cay. There was so much wind that we had to reef, and then later drop the main. Even then we were tearing along in that shallow water at close to eight knots. After the deep water and gentle breezes of the Pacific, all this seemed like very energetic cruising. We anchored in Allen's small harbor with two anchors, both rodes out of the bow chock. The anchors were set in an almost straight line. One was dropped as *Loon* sailed in, then we sailed on, paying out the first line, and dropped the second one. After getting sail off, we pulled *Loon* back so that she was in the middle between the two anchors. The point of this so-called Bahamian moor is that your swinging circle is very small, and in the tiny coves in the Bahamas, this leaves room for more boats. It's especially important here, since the tidal currents are often strong, and boats of different shapes and drafts lie at different angles to the tide and wind. The Bahamian moor is another example of local conditions producing strange (to us outlanders) but appropriate and effective ways of doing things.

We spent a day with the local conch sloops at Allen Cay as we all waited out a blow, then had a long sail across the Yellow Bank to Nassau, where we arranged to leave *Loon* for a while in the totally enclosed small pond called Hurricane Hole on Paradise Island. This is just across from Nassau itself and makes up one side of that long narrow harbor. Sally had to fly home the next day, but the boys and I were somewhat delayed, in part because of the enormous amount of possessions they had collected in their three years of cruising. In those days, U.S. Customs inspection was in Nassau. When the inspector saw Al and Dick's *thirty* cardboard boxes lined up for inspection, all tied up with rope, he was aghast, but ended up not opening a single one. It was a sad day when Dick and Al finally left us. They had turned out to be a wonderful addition to our crew, and we were to enjoy many more happy passages and cruises together over the coming years.

In June I came back with Sally and our son Sandy to bring *Loon* the rest of the way home. We expected Danny Walker to arrive on the morning of June 6, but he didn't show up. Thinking one of us might have mistaken the date, we waited another day and a couple of hours for good measure, but he still didn't appear, so the three of us took off without him.

The next two days were busy ones for us, shorthanded as we were. There was a lot of careful navigation to do to make sure we were safely around the northern Bahamas, and we had one thundersquall after another, which meant a lot of sail handling. Near evening on the second day out, while we were still in the Gulf Stream, I saw what looked like a raft on the horizon. Sure enough, that's what it was. I thought at first it must be some crazy man trying to sail across the Atlantic in the most unsuitable possible vessel, since there had been a rash of such adventures at that time. But as we approached, we saw that there were three men and a young boy on the raft, which was made of two gas tanks with a cabin ladder and some planks lashed over them to make a platform and hold them together. What had looked like a small mast from a distance turned out to be a radio aerial sticking out of one of the gas tanks' fill pipes.

The people didn't wave or yell, but when I asked if they wanted help, they said they would like to be picked up. As I turned downwind to shoot up alongside, one of them said anxiously, "Don't go away, Mister." I wasn't about to. We came alongside, and without any obvious urgency they joined us on *Loon*.

They were a strange lot. The boy, about twelve, wore a giveaway Eastern Airlines cap, and the men had on thick-soled, high-laced black shoes. They had a satchel filled with food, a big jug of water, and some fishing equipment. They certainly didn't seem euphoric, or even particularly pleased about being rescued. Their story, told by the boy's father (only he and the boy spoke at all), was that they were on their way to Grand Bahama in a new twin-screw Hatteras powerboat, when a squall came up and the boat started sinking. They were able to pry the gas tanks out from beneath the cockpit with some two-by-fours that they happened to have on board and build the raft over the side, while the boat obligingly took four hours to finish sinking. They were unable, in four hours, to find the leak. Their electric bilge pump couldn't keep up with the slow leak, and they didn't have a manual backup. Their dinghy had been stolen the night before they set out, and their radio wasn't working.

The whole story seemed ludicrous. There were no obvious marks on their hands, and it seemed almost impossible that anyone could have built that raft alongside a boat in a sea big enough to sink it without someone getting at least some mashed fingers. The boy and his father spoke with a very marked Carolina accent, and the other two appeared to be foreigners, though they said practically nothing. When they asked to be taken to Cape Kennedy, where there was no Customs and Immigration Office, I became even more suspicious.

We told them we'd take them to West Palm Beach and started there under power, since we had to buck the Gulf Stream and the breeze was light. They refused food, and didn't even want to go below at first, but Sandy finally took them there and put them in bunks, where they spent the night, never offering to give us a hand or even coming on deck again until we reached harbor. Even in those days I was worried that they might try to highjack *Loon,* but there wasn't much we could do about it, since at that time we didn't have a radio transmitter. I considered going on watch wearing my pistol, but this seemed almost too ridiculous, and, perhaps unwisely, I decided not to. I did wear a sheath knife, but this wouldn't have helped much against three determined men. It was a very long and uneasy night.

When the men emerged from the cabin the next morning, there

were no friendly greetings, no "good morning"—they just sat down on the rail and muttered in low voices to each other. When we got into harbor, they started ashore with a brief and somewhat surly "Thanks, Cap," until I made it clear that they damn well better wait for Customs and Immigration or take the consequences. After that they settled down reluctantly to scrambled eggs and bacon on deck. This was fortunate for us, because if they had gone ashore without the proper formalities, we would most likely have been fined for letting them go. The officials, when they finally arrived at nine, were rude to them, but once our castaways produced driver's licenses the government men were uninterested. A woman in a rusty station wagon came to pick them up, and that was the end of that. I reported the incident and the abandoned raft to an officer of a Coast Guard vessel in the harbor, but he was equally uninterested.

The three of us had a rough sail around Cape Hatteras to Morehead City with a big bunch of very friendly porpoises who played around *Loon* for an hour on the last day. This was the first time we had heard their clicks and squeaks through the hull as they played under the bow, but since then we've heard their echolocation noises—and perhaps conversation—many times, now that we know what to listen for.

There was more excitement going into Morehead City, with a strong onshore wind and a fair tide. We might not have dared go in through the heavy surf that would have been created with an ebbing tide running against the wind in that shallow entrance; as it was there was heavy surf in the shallower water on both sides of the channel. Then we were faced with a new bridge to go under before we could reach the Inland Waterway. It wasn't on the old chart we had borrowed from friends in Nassau, but I thought I remembered that all bridges across the waterway had to have 55 feet of clearance at high water and that we'd be OK because *Loon*'s masthead is 54½ feet above the water. I was wrong—the bridge has only a 50-foot clearance at high tide. Fortunately, the tide wasn't all the way in, and we made it, but only just. It was plenty scary approaching that bridge, with the Kenyon reading eight knots and a strong fair tide under us. In retrospect, that episode is something I'm not very proud of. Maybe we could have made it under the bridge even at high tide because *Loon* was heeled, but it was really a stupid chance to take. We should have taken off sail and approached slowly under power.

We left *Loon* at Beaufort for a couple of weeks before coming back with our dachshund, Sam, to sail up the waterway to Gibson Island, where we had kept her before our Pacific cruise. Before we left, we called Dan Walker and found that he had mistaken the day (or maybe we had) and had arrived at Nassau just in time to see us sail out of the harbor. With his usual ingenuity, he had found a berth on a catamaran and sailed to West Palm Beach, arriving, again, shortly after we left. Then he sailed on to Morehead City, where he was tied up in another marina when we sailed in, but this time he didn't see us. We had just missed each other by the narrowest of margins all along the way.

Our trip home up the waterway was often beautiful, but hard on Sam, who was a very well housebroken character, and absolutely refused to relieve his bladder on any beaches. He was an inland dog, used to grass, not sand, and he insisted on holding out for hours before peeing on the foredeck, much ashamed in spite of our efforts to reassure him that it was all right. He even refused to use a small island, where I cut down a patch of coarse, spiky grass with a machete for him. Only the smooth lawns at the two locks we went through, and the towns where we tied up were civilized enough for him.

When we got to the Chesapeake, we were met by a thunderstorm that gave plenty of warning, with a white roll cloud at its leading edge and a nasty pink color behind that. It lived up to its advertising. I took down the main before it arrived, but it blew so hard that the working jib was too much for her, and I had to get this off at the height of the blow. By this time it was raining so hard that we could see the crests of only two seas looking downwind, and the driven rain made it too painful to look upwind at all.

Loon hove to fine with just the mizzen on, reaching very slowly ahead and making a little leeway. When the blow was over, a big menhaden fishing boat that we had seen before the squall started over our way to see if we were all right, but turned away when he saw me hoisting the jib again. We thought it was very friendly of him to want to make sure we were OK.

We sailed on into Reedsville, the home of many of the menhaden boats and the site of a plant that extracts the oil and makes the rest into fertilizer. It was an attractive-looking anchorage, but the aroma was just too much to bear. After a walk ashore for Sam and a good look around to make sure the thunderstorms had gone, we moved from the smelly, complete protection of Reedsville to a less sheltered but much less aromatic anchorage for the night.

We reached our slip at Gibson Island, and shortly after that headed for New England. Sailing up the New Jersey beach on the way, with our daughter and a couple of friends from the lab as crew, we met another thundersquall. It came with a white roll

Mizzenmast overboard

cloud in front, like the one off Reedsville. I hove *Loon* to with just the mizzen, as before. It soon became apparent that this was not just a real screecher, it was the granddaddy of all thunder-squalls. In the middle of it there was a sudden let-up. *Loon* fell off, a tremendous puff hit her, and the top half of the mizzen went over the side. The upper shroud had pulled off the top half of its chain plate at deck level. The mast broke in two places—just above the spreaders and at the partners. We were just beginning to clean up the mess when we saw another black cloud in a solid line parallel to the beach, stretching out of sight in both directions. It was really ugly, and we didn't know what was going to happen next. We rushed to cut off the sail, pull the pins in the rigging, and get the shrouds coiled and the pieces of the mast snugged down on board before this one arrived. We barely finished in time. If the last one was bad, this one looked far worse. What it produced was only a moderately strong breeze. I was right when I decided years before that I couldn't tell how hard a squall was going to blow. We learned later that the squalls that day had blown down several barns in New Jersey.

As we sailed *Loon,* now looking very strange in her sloop rig, through New York Harbor and the familiar waters of Long Island Sound, we couldn't help thinking how odd it was that the only damage she received on the long trip to the South Pacific and back took place in home waters, only a few miles from where she had been built by Jakobson in Oyster Bay. But that's how that Pacific cruise ended—the closer we got to home the scarier it got.

In spite of the relatively minor matter of losing the mizzen, we were pleased to have carried out another long voyage successfully and very happily, without any of the crew problems, groundings, and other disasters that so frequently crop up in many similar voyages. People (fortunately, not my publishers) often ask, "Didn't you have *any* close brushes with really dangerous situations—no shipwrecks, strandings, cannibalistic natives, shark attacks, tropical diseases; no threat of piracy, or of succumbing to the lure of beautiful Polynesian nymphomaniacs—*no real excitement* to tell or write about?" The answer is, yes, we did have real excitement.

But out-of-control situations, disasters, and near-misses are not the marks of a well-run ship, and we have enough pride not to exaggerate the minor problems and thrills into major proportions. If it all makes for a dull sea story, so be it. Most sailors know that the biggest thrills come from doing things competently, not from blundering into situations where they—or others—are put in danger and have to be rescued.

14

We've heard people say after a long cruise that they were fed up with sailing and were going to give it up for a life ashore. One round-the-world sailor we met in Panama said he was through with "zig-zag sailing" and was either going to buy a powerboat or stay ashore; in any case, he couldn't wait to get home and begin. We didn't feel that way. Twenty years later we're still sailing *Loon* along the coast to Maine and Nova Scotia. We've returned with her to the Caribbean. We've taken her to visit Europe via the Azores. Together we've been to Ireland, Scotland, Norway, Denmark, Sweden, and Finland, and returned home by way of Germany, Holland, England, Madeira, and Bermuda. I've also taken to building boats and am currently near finishing a copy of a 25-foot Nat Herreshoff steam launch in my garage, but that's a story for another time. I suppose it all just shows that when some people start an affair with boats and the sea, they're stuck with it.

Sailing and racing have had a wonderful effect on Sally's and my life together. It's something we've always done as a team, totally relying on each other, and sharing the problems, dangers, and frequent joys and euphoria together. Reporters have sometimes asked Sally for the "woman's point of view" about our cruises and races, but for us there really isn't a woman's or a man's point of view. There is a single desire, and that is to do the job and do it with style. To this end we obviously have different skills and weaknesses. I'm physically stronger than she, and do more of the foredeck work, but by no means all. She is more meticulous than I, and a much better navigator, but she asks me to take sights to check hers on important landfalls. (She often has to brush me up on working them out.) She's a better light-weather helmsman and can make the boat really go, but she hates to steer downwind with a spinnaker on when it's blowing hard. We work together, trying to maximize our combined efforts by the best use of our own strengths, which don't necessarily split on conventional male-female lines.

Sailing also gives a tremendous sense of accomplishment that the crew earns together. With a good and compatible crew on a long passage or race, the intense feeling of unity, satisfaction, and serenity extends to the whole operation, and ego problems get left behind. In my own experience, this is unique to sailing, but I'm sure it occurs in other groups with a common goal whose members depend on and trust each other completely. It's an experience well worth having and produces extraordinary happiness and elation. It's a wonderful feeling to be handling sail on the foredeck in a hard blow with an intelligent, skillful, and trusted helmsman backing you up in the cockpit—trying to keep you as dry as possible, easing the boat to make your job simpler, and thinking ahead so as to be ready with any help required.

Racing doesn't give the extreme sense of peace that a long offshore passage can, but it certainly does provide the same trust and unity in pursuing a single goal. It can even be relaxing after the tension of the preparation and start—no more shopping for things you can't get, no more frantic last-minute repairs, no more worry about collisions at the starting line—now all there is to do is enjoy sailing the boat as fast as she will go.

After all these years, what advice would I give to young sailors wanting to sail to foreign shores? I think first it would be: If you want a happy sailing life, marry a sailor. If you're not lucky enough to have done that, do your best to make your wife or husband enjoy it by giving them a real part in the fun that they can excel at. Navigation, for example, is a skill that can be acquired, where hard work, meticulousness, and attention to detail pay off. It's a vital part of the operation and can be handled by someone without the physical strength needed on the foredeck. Hesitant sailors should be encouraged to do whatever they like to do and make it their specialty.

The same thing applies to the crew. Make them feel that they are essential to the success of the race or cruise—which they are. If the crew isn't happy, the skipper isn't going to be either. So many men, when they get on a boat as skipper, become rude, sarcastic, and dictatorial, apparently believing that behaving with decent manners and consideration isn't important afloat and will be regarded by the crew as a sign of weakness. Actually, in the crowded conditions on a small boat, consideration for others is much more important than it is ashore, where there's more privacy and therefore less chance of getting on each other's nerves. There's nothing that can spoil a race or cruise faster or more completely than hurt feelings and resentment—so whether you're skipper or crew, do everything you can to keep things friendly and happy with the others on board.

If you ask your crew's advice, you may find that you learn a lot, but even if you don't, you'll make them happy and a far better crew than if you snub them. If you compliment them on a job well done, you will get better work out of them than by criticizing them for a badly done job. If you have to express your displeasure, aim it at the job done rather than at the person doing it, and try not to be angry and sarcastic about it. Make a joke of it, if you can. Sometimes I find it hard to criticize before I'm really mad but I know it's much better to do it earlier and in a friendly manner. Delegate when you can. This is only common sense and skillful administration, and that's what a skipper is—not a god, just an administrator (with, let's hope, a few other skills in addition).

We've always run a democratic operation on our boats, but this doesn't mean that consensus rules. What it does mean is that until I say "OK, that's what we'll do," discussion and advice are welcomed and listened to. After that they aren't. Obviously, someone has to make the final decisions if the ship is going to be happy and well run, but you don't have to be either unpleasant or stupid about it. Crew morale is a very precious thing. Look out for it. Obvious as this is, many skippers spend little thought on it.

A good crew also gives the skipper support. After all, he's human too, and doesn't need argument after a decision has been made; nor does he need recrimination over past mistakes from the benefit of hindsight. There's no point in worrying over past errors—everyone makes them. The important thing is to race or cruise to the finish line as well as you can from where you are now, not from where you should have been if you hadn't made a mistake.

Another thing we feel very strongly about is sailing with a sense of style—that is, do it as well as you can, and learn to do it better as time goes by. It means doing things precisely, and, if possible, with a certain amount of grace. Even showing off a little is OK, if you don't overextend yourself and goof. Most of all, it means stretching your skill by taking minor chances that raise your pulse a bit, rather than doing it the easy way each time—sailing to your mooring or into a dock or slip, for instance. Many people motor in and out of harbor by habit, and miss the thrill of leaving under sail and coming to anchor smartly. Granted, many harbors are too crowded for the tyro to make and leave his mooring under sail, but there are less crowded places to practice, and knowing how to handle your boat in tight situations without an engine may well come in handy someday. It certainly has for us many times.

Sally and I have a technique for sailing off the anchor that we think saves a lot of effort compared to the standard procedure of pulling the boat over it by hand, and then trying to free it by brute strength. With the main hoisted and Sally at the helm, I pay out enough anchor cable for *Loon* to fall off and start sailing. When she has sailed far enough so that we can fetch the anchor on the other tack (allowing for the catenary, or curve in the rode, as it is pulled sideways through the water), we tack and sail to the anchor with plenty of way on. I take up slack on the line as we go, and when it's straight up and down I snub it quickly. If there's a reasonable breeze, the boat's momentum plucks the anchor out of the bottom easily. Sally can tell that the anchor is free when *Loon*'s bow dips, and she heads up to slow down while I pull the anchor up into its roller; then she lets *Loon* fall off and start sailing. The whole job of getting under way is done with a minimum of effort and gives us the advantage of knowing which tack we'll be on when the anchor comes up. This is safer than pulling the boat up to the anchor head to wind, and not being sure which way she'll fall off when free of the bottom.

Knowing how to handle your boat without all the fancy electronic aids that have been developed over the years will also give you satisfaction. We only bought a radio transmitter after we had owned *Loon* for several years and didn't get Loran until 1984. These are all, I'm sure, very useful gadgets, but they do break down, and an ability to get where you want to go without them can be very useful when that happens.

To us, the essence of getting the most out of sailing is to put yourself in a position of some risk—an offshore passage for instance, where you rely only on your crew, your boat and its preparation, and your own skills to make the difference between success and failure. Skill is the important word—we value it and try very hard to increase it. To us, this is living in contact with reality, unlike the world ashore, where most of us deal with many of our problems by paying someone else to handle them for us. Offshore there simply isn't anyone to do anything for you—you really are on your own, and totally alive.

There's a school of thought that doesn't feel it's worth learning the many skills involved in sailing, but the whole point, fun, and satisfaction of the exercise, in our view, is being self-sufficient. Making repairs and improvements ourselves on *Loon* is a large part of the fun for us. Splicing, whipping, varnishing, carpentry, and engine repairs are all skills that make sailing more fun and reduce your dependence on others. The more independent you are, the more real your adventures become.

There is nothing particularly difficult about sailing or racing. If you're a beginner, the terminology seems unnecessarily complicated and off-putting, but, in fact, when you learn it, is the simplest way to say what you want to say, and say it quickly. It takes a while to absorb the lingo and learn the skills, but all the sailors before you had to start as beginners and learn it all too. There's no mystery about it: it's mainly common sense decked out in new language.

Careful preparation of the boat, yourself, and the crew is the greatest safety factor of all. For a long voyage, especially if it's offshore, it's a very good idea to have your crew checked out by their doctors before starting, and get their advice about what to do if troubles arise. Similarly, the boat should be thoroughly gone over. Make sure the rigging is in good shape, with no tiny cracks in the swaged fittings, or worn Norsemen fittings if you have those, or, on older boats, corroded plow steel wire or bad splices. Make sure the rudder fittings are in good shape, and that the fire extinguishers have been recently checked. Be sure you have planned carefully and have taken enough water (in separate tanks), food, and the necessary spares and tools, as well as medical equipment and a first-aid book. These are just a few of the many things to think about and check over as you prepare for the trip or race.

It's important to be on the very best terms with your yard and the men in it, if you're not doing all your own work. Compliments are much more effective than criticism in getting good work done quickly. Paying your bills on time and being pleasant with the people working on your boat will pay big dividends in getting a good job done and may well make your bills cheaper than they otherwise would be. Besides, you'll get to be friends with some very interesting and highly skilled people, from whom you can learn a lot.

There are those in the yachting game who brag that they have stolen their boats out from under the yard's security precautions to avoid paying a bill that they felt was unjustified. People who have a reputation for fairness and paying their just bills on time don't find their boats chained to the slip when they come to get them and don't have to sneak in at night with a hacksaw in order to sail home. In my experience, owners of that breed are also the ones who complain that their engines only last a couple of years, their radios don't work, and the rigging is poorly done. Well-cared-for engines often last twenty years or more. *Loon* has all the same standing rigging, except for a head stay, that she was built with twenty-three years ago. If you are fair with the yard, they are much more apt to take good care of your boat, which in turn will take good care of you.

Finally, I can't do better than pass on some advice my father gave me many years ago. He convinced me that taking on adventure was one of man's most important obligations, as well as being a source of great satisfaction. You can always find plenty of reasons for following the conventional safe and easy path, but if you do, you will miss some of the very best of life, and never even know it.

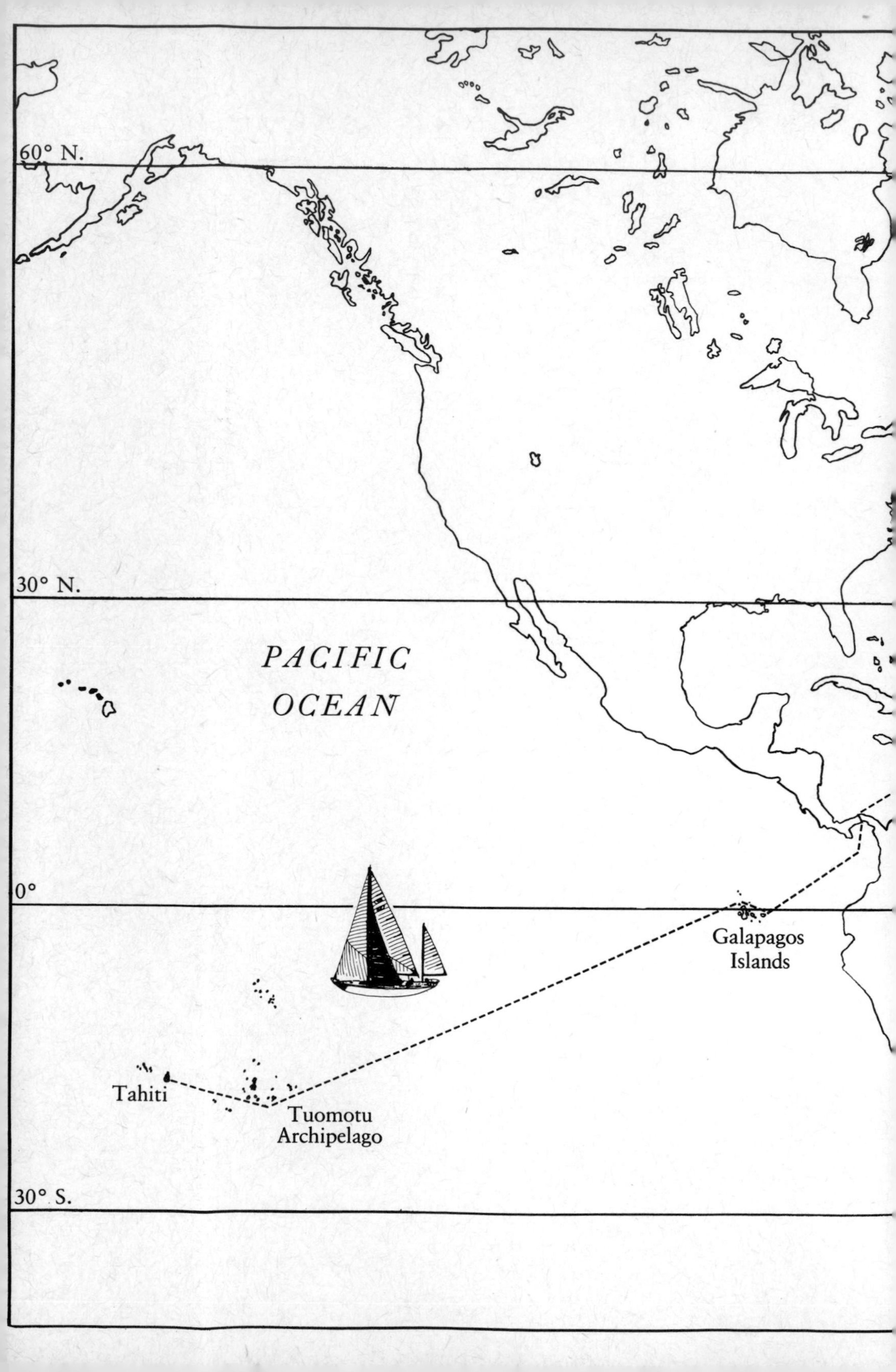
60° N.
30° N.
PACIFIC
OCEAN
0°
Galapagos
Islands
Tahiti
Tuomotu
Archipelago
30° S.